BLESS ME, ULTIMA

Rudolfo Anaya

AUTHORED by Caitlin Vincent
UPDATED AND REVISED by Soman Chainani

COVER DESIGN by Table XI Partners LLC
COVER PHOTO by Olivia Verma and © 2005 GradeSaver, LLC

BOOK DESIGN by Table XI Partners LLC

Published by GradeSaver LLC, www.gradesaver.com

First published in the United States of America by GradeSaver LLC. 2008

GRADESAVER, the GradeSaver logo and the phrase "Getting you the grade since 1999" are registered trademarks of GradeSaver, LLC

ISBN 978-1-60259-135-6

Printed in the United States of America

For other products and additional information please visit
http://www.gradesaver.com

Table of Contents

Table of Contents

Biography of Rudolfo Anaya (1937-)

Rudolfo Alfonso Anaya was born on October 30, 1937 in Pastura, New Mexico, the fifth of seven children. His father, Martin Anaya, was a cowboy who worked on ranches in the surrounding areas, while his mother, Rafaelita, was devoutly Catholic and came from a family of poor farmers. Shortly after his birth, Anaya's family moved to Santa Rosa, a small town in the Pecos River valley, where he spent most of his childhood. Anaya's time in the Santa Rosa community was extremely influential for his writing: many of his novels contain images, characters, and myths from the New Mexican culture that he experienced as a child. His family moved to Albuquerque when Anaya was fifteen, and he was forced to adapt to an entirely new culture very different from the close-knit community of his youth.

At the age of sixteen, Anaya was forced into a lengthy convalescence after suffering a severe diving accident that broke two of the vertebrae in his neck. He spent an entire summer in the hospital but eventually recovered and was able to regain his active lifestyle. This near-death experience was quite influential for him and appears in a different form in Bless Me, Ultima when the character of Florence dies in a swimming accident.

Anaya graduated from high school in Albuquerque in 1956 and began to attend Browning Business School with the intention of becoming an accountant. After deciding that the life of an accountant was not for him, Anaya enrolled at the University of New Mexico and took a freshman English course that sparked his enthusiasm for literature. He began to experiment with writing poetry and short stories and eventually graduated with a Bachelors degree in English in 1963.

From 1963 to 1970, Anaya worked as a public school teacher in junior high school. After spending each day teaching, Anaya would return home and spend the evening writing and struggling to find a unique literary voice. According to Anaya, during one of these evenings of writing, he turned around to see a vision of an elderly woman dressed in black: a mystical figure that would become the character of Ultima in his first novel. With the encouragement of his wife, who he married in 1966, and the inspiration of his vision, Anaya began to work on Bless Me, Ultima. The book took several years and several drafts to complete, and, even after its completion, it was rejected repeatedly by East Coast publishers for being too "Latino" in style. Finally, the manuscript was accepted and published by Quinto Sol, a small press in Berkeley. The book was awarded the Premio Quinto Sol Literary prize for the best Chicano novel of the year and quickly became a classic work in Chicano literature.

In 1974, Anaya took a teaching position at the University of New Mexico, one that he held until his retirement in 1993. He published his second novel, Heart of Aztlan, in 1976 and his third novel, Tortuga, in 1979, completing a loosely autobiographical trilogy of New Mexican culture that began with Bless Me, Ultima. After the completion of his trilogy, Anaya began to publish poems, short stories, theater pieces, and children's stories, including The Silence of the Llano (1982), La Legend of La Llorona (1984), and The Adventures of Juan Chicaspatas (1985). In 1992, he began to work on another series of novels, including Alburquerque (1995), Zia Summer (1995), Rio Grande Fall (1996), and Shaman Winter (1999).

Over the course of his writing career, Anaya has received several prestigious awards, including the Before Columbus Book Award (1980), the New Mexico Governor's Award for Excellence and Achievement in Literature (1980), the Award for Achievement in Chicano Literature (1983), the Mexican Medal of Friendship from the Mexican Consulate (1986), the PEN-West Fiction Award (1992), and the National Medal of Arts from President George Bush (2002). He currently lives in Albuquerque with his wife.

About Bless Me, Ultima

Bless Me, Ultima is a semi-autobiographical novel based on the New Mexican community of Rudolfo Anaya's childhood. Anaya used his memory of his town, the Pecos River, Highway 66, the church, the school, and the surrounding villages and ranches as the inspiration for their depiction in his novel. Anaya also created clear similarities between the characters in the book and the characters in his childhood. Antonio's parents are based loosely on Anaya's parents: his father was a vaquero who was raised on the llano, and his mother grew up in a community of Catholic farmers. Anaya's brothers were fighting in World War II for most of his childhood in the same way that Antonio's three older brothers are fighting overseas in the novel. Moreover, similar to Antonio's family and their treatment of Ultima in the novel, Anaya's family was extremely respectful of the role played by the curandera in their community, reconciling the importance of folk medicine with their Catholic faith.

In addition to its ties to Anaya's personal experiences and background, Bless Me, Ultima also relates to the larger historical and cultural issues surrounding New Mexico. A Spanish colony beginning in 1695, New Mexico was initially colonized for the purpose of converting the native Pueblo Indians. The Spanish built permanent communities for the Indians along the Rio Grande and introduced domesticated animals to the area, all while striving for religious conversion of the native communities. The Spanish recruited the native people to build mission churches in each of the new villages, but the Pueblo Indians finally rebelled in 1680 and drove the Spanish out of their land.

In 1692, the Spanish, led by Don Diego de Vargas, conquered New Mexico once more. This time, however, the colonizers were able to coexist successfully with the Pueblo Indians and established many communities in which Catholicism and Spanish language was combined with the culture and myths of the Pueblo Indians. New Mexico gained independence from Spain in 1821 and eventually achieved independent statehood in the United States of American in 1910. However, the blended culture of the Spanish and the Pueblo Indians remained largely intact in small New Mexican villages for the first half of the 20th century.

In Bless Me, Ultima, this amalgamation of cultures is extremely apparent: the descendants of the Pueblo Indians still live according to a unique faith drawn from ancient native beliefs and Catholic doctrine and continue to farm the land as their livelihood. Moreover, Spanish remains the primary language, with Antonio only learning English after he begins to go to school.

During the 1960s and 1970s, at the time that Anaya began to write Bless Me, Ultima, the Mexican American population was finally beginning to flourish as an individual artistic community. In this period, known as the Chicano Movement, poetry, literature, music, and theater began to become integral parts of Mexican American culture, independent from the general culture of the United States. This movement was seen as a way to improve the economic and social lives of the Mexican American community while simultaneously rooting it in its own history and creativity. Because Anaya was one of the first authors to promote this unique culture in his novels, he is recognized by many to be the "father" of Chicano literature.

Character List

Antonio "Tony" Márez

Antonio is six years old at the beginning of the novel. He is at the center of a conflict between the Márez values of his father and the Luna beliefs of his mother; while his father would like him to become a cowboy, his mother desperately wants him to become a priest. He works as an apprentice to Ultima, absorbing her wisdom about life and learning the characteristics and names of herbs and plants she uses in his work. Over the course of the novel, Antonio experiences several tragedies that make him question the meaning of sin and morality and the truth of religion. Eventually, he determines to find his own path in life and create his own religious faith.

Ultima

Ultima is the elderly curandera, or healer, who comes to live with the Márez family at the invitation of Antonio's mother. She learned her powers from a great healer called the Flying Man in Las Pasturas. Although Ultima is ultimately good, she is greatly feared by those who do not understand her power and is accused of being a bruja, or witch. She teaches Antonio her wisdom about life and her faith in the power of the earth and the river. She is represented by an owl that contains her spirit.

Gabriel Márez

Gabriel is Antonio's father who wants his son to follow in his footsteps and spend his days roaming the llano on horseback. After Antonio was born, Maria convinced Gabriel to leave his life on the llano and move the family to the town of Guadalupe for the chance at a new life. Although Gabriel tried to please his wife, he was unable to rid himself of his love for the llano. He takes a job on the highway, but loses the respect of the other vaqueros and develops a serious drinking problem. While Maria constantly pressures Antonio to become a priest, Gabriel never tries to persuade his son to become a vaquero but only wants him to make his own choices. His one remaining dream is to move to California, the "land of milk and honey," but his dream never becomes a reality.

Maria Luna y Márez

Antonio's mother and a close friend of Ultima's. She is the daughter of farmers from El Puerto de los Lunas. Devoutly Catholic, she desperately wants Antonio to become a priest of the Luna instead of a vaquero like his father.

Andrew "Andy" Márez

Andrew is the second son of Gabriel and Maria, has a special relationship with Antonio. He returns from World War II and stays behind in Guadalupe when his other brothers leave with the intention of studying for his high school diploma.

However, Andrew is unable to maintain his goal and begins to yearn to leave. Andrew forever changes Antonio's idealized perception of him when Antonio observes Andrew at Rosie's with a prostitute. Instead of helping Narciso protect Ultima from Tenorio, Andrew chooses to remain with the prostitute, and Narciso ends up dying because of it. After Eugene and León return from Las Vegas, Andrew quits his job at Allen's Market and move to Santa Fe with them.

Eugene "Gene" Márez

Eugene is the third son of Gabriel and Maria and the leader of the three older boys. He fights overseas in World War II with his two brothers and returns to Guadalupe, anxious to start a new life in a new city. After spending his war pension at the pool hall of Guadalupe with his brothers, he moves to Las Vegas with León. Eventually, he and León return home during a blizzard and take Andrew to Santa Fe with them.

León Márez

León is Antonio's eldest brother. He also fights in World War II and, suffering from the "war sickness," has terrible nightmares of war. He and Eugene leave together to seek their fortune in Las Vegas and return to Guadalupe only to take Andrew to Santa Fe with them.

Deborah Márez

Deborah is Antonio's older sister. She has been studying at school for two years and prefers speaking English to speaking Spanish. Antonio's mother fears that she has too much Márez blood in her.

Theresa Márez

Theresa is younger than Deborah and learns English from her. Theresa spends all of her time playing dolls with Deborah.

Narciso

Narciso is known as the town drunk. He is close friends with Gabriel because they share a love for the llano. Maria also approves of Narciso, despite his drinking, because he helped her when she was giving birth to her daughters. Although Narciso is technically a vaquero, he is able to create a compromise between his cowboy mentality and the lifestyle of a Luna farmer and grows a beautiful garden outside of his house. Narciso also has a great deal of affection for Ultima and warns the Marez family whenever she is in danger. He is ultimately murdered by Tenorio because he tries to protect Ultima.

Tenorio Trementina

Tenorio Trementina is an evil saloon-keeper and barber who lives in El Puerto. His three daughters are witches who place a curse on Lucas Luna. After Ultima lifts the curse and Tenorio's daughter begin to die, Tenorio swears to take revenge on Ultima. He spends the rest of the novel trying to murder her and kills Narciso when he gets in Tenorio's way. Tenorio eventually succeeds in killing Ultima when he shoots her owl familiar. Tenorio's hatred of Ultima highlights the conflict between good and evil that is present throughout the book.

The Trementina sisters

The three daughters of Tenorio are witches or brujas. They place a curse on Lucas Luna after he interrupts them while they are performing a Black Mass. After Ultima lifts the curse on Lucas Luna, the first Trementina sister falls sick and dies. Shortly afterwards, the second Trementina sister falls sick and dies, prompting Tenorio to attack Ultima.

Lupito

Lupito is a war veteran suffering from the "war sickness." In his insanity, he murders the sheriff of Guadalupe and is later shot to death by a mob beneath the town bridge while Antonio watches. Lupito's murder is the first death that Antonio observes, and it has a profound affect on him, prompting his questions about death, sin, and morality for the rest of the book.

Téllez

Téllez is a friend of Antonio's father. He seeks Ultima's help in alleviating the curse that is afflicting his home and family.

Cico

Cico is a friend of Antonio's and takes him to visit the Golden Carp during the summer. He does not hang out with Antonio's other friends and prefers to spend his time fishing alone. He tells Antonio the apocalyptic prophecy of the Golden Carp and the legend of the mermaids who live in the Hidden Lakes.

Florence

Florence is one of Antonio's friends. Florence is an atheist because he cannot reconcile the injustices in the world with a loving and compassionate God. The primary reason for his atheism is his difficult background: his mother died when she was three, his father drank himself to death, and both of his sisters work as prostitutes in Rosie's brothel. He still attends catechism but only so that he can be with his friends. Although Antonio tries to argue against Florence's cynicism, he is unable to deny Florence's logical reasoning; Florence forces Antonio to acknowledge that every religion has flaws. Florence dies near the end of the book in a swimming accident.

Samuel

Samuel is one of Antonio's close friends. He seems to be very old and wise, and he tells Antonio the story of the Golden Carp.

Jasón Chavéz

Jasón is one of Antonio's friends. He disobeys his father and continues to visit the Indian who lives in the hills near the town.

Horse, Red, Bones, Abel, Lloyd, Willie, the Vitamin Kid, Ernie, and others

Antonio's classmates and friends. Horse has bad breath and loves to wrestle. Red is a Protestant and is teased by his friends because of it. Bones is the most intimidating of Antonio's friends because he acts as if he is insane. Abel is the smallest of Antonio's friend and has a tendency to urinate at inopportune times. The Vitamin Kid is the fastest runner in Guadalupe. He is Samuel's brother, and no one knows his real name. Ernie loves to brag and constantly reminds his friends that they can be sued for any minor infraction.

Juan Luna

Juan Luna is one of Antonio's uncles who lives at El Puerto. He is very quiet and reserved like the other Luna farmers.

Mateo Luna

Mateo Luna is one of Antonio's uncles who lives at El Puerto. He is the best story teller in the family.

Pedro Luna

Pedro Luna is Antonio's favorite uncle. He teaches Antonio the ways of the Luna when Antonio spends the summer farming at El Puerto. Pedro shoots Tenorio when he is about to kill Antonio.

Lucas Luna

Lucas is the youngest of the Luna brothers. He is cursed by the Trementina sisters after observing them perform a Black Mass. Ultima cures him, and he swears to return the favor if she ever needs his help.

Prudencio Luna

Prudencio Luna is Antonio's grandfather on his mother's side. He is very quiet and reserved and does not want his sons to become involved in the conflict between Tenorio and Ultima.

Father Byrnes

Father Byrnes gives Antonio and his friends their lessons in catechism to prepare them for their first communion. He is very stern and hypocritical and prefers that his students remain ignorant of God so that they will fear Him.

Rosie

Rosie is the owner of the local brothel in town. All of Antonio's brothers frequently visit the brothel, and Antonio experiences a great deal of personal anxiety about their lust and seeming immorality.

Chavéz

Chavéz is Jasón's father and the brother of the sheriff who Lupito kills. He tells Gabriel Márez about the murder and rounds up a mob to hunt and kill Lupito. He does not approve of his son's friendship with the Indian and orders Jasón to stop seeing him, an order which Jasón ignores.

Jasón Chavéz's Indian

Jasón Chavéz's Indian lives near the town. According to Cico, was the first person to tell him the story of the Golden Carp.

Miss Maestas

Miss Maestas is Antonio's first grade teacher. Antonio excels in her class, and she promotes him to the third grade at the end of the year.

The Flying Man

The Flying Man, or "el hombre volador," is Ultima's teacher. He gave her the owl that became her familiar and the guardian of her spirit. His name still inspires respect among those who have heard of his power, and Ultima invokes his name to frighten Tenorio.

Miss Violet

Miss Violet is Antonio's third grade teacher and one of the organizers of the disastrous Christmas Play.

Benito Campos

Benito is a good friend of Gabriel Marez's. When Gabriel moved to Guadalupe and gave up his vaquero life, Benito took Gabriel's horse and allowed it to roam free on the llano.

Major Themes

Loss of Innocence

One of the major themes of the novel is Antonio's loss of innocence. At the opening of the novel, Antonio is an innocent boy, unaware of the dangers and tragedy of life. As the novel progresses, Antonio becomes more and more cognizant of the good and evil present in the world. By the end of the book, Antonio no longer possesses his innocence but has replaced it with wisdom and maturity.

Antonio's transition from innocence to experience is highlighted through specific trials over the course of the novel. The first of these trials is Lupito's murder, which sparks Antonio's anxieties about sin and punishment. The murder of Narciso is another key moment in the novel, forcing Antonio to witness yet another death and also assume the role of a priest to give the dying man comfort. The remainder of Antonio's innocence is lost with the accidental drowning of Florence. One of Antonio's closest friends, Florence constantly reminded Antonio that a compassionate God could not exist in such an evil world. With his death, Antonio begins to question whether or not he can believe in a God who could allow Florence to die.

As Antonio feels the loss of his innocence, he looks to religion to answer his concerns. He hopes that his first communion will finally answer all of his questions but is disappointed when God remains silent to him. Feeling betrayed by the Christian God, Antonio looks to the Golden Carp and Ultima's skills to help him reconcile his loss of innocence with his development as a young man. Antonio's mother associates the loss of innocence with sin and corruption, but Antonio eventually understands that loss of innocence is a crucial part of growing up.

Conflicting Cultures

Anaya uses his novel to introduce the reader to several conflicting cultures in Antonio's childhood. First of all, Antonio's early life is defined by the conflict between the Luna and the Marez, the two sides of his family. While the Luna are devout farmers who worship the earth and the moon, the Marez are free-spirited cowboys who are devoted to horses and the sun. Because Antonio's three older brothers have already chosen the roaming life of the Marez, Antonio is expected to follow the path of the Luna and become a priest. However, Antonio is unwilling to make a decision either way and feels a great deal of pressure weighing on his destiny. Eventually, Ultima teaches Antonio that identity can be a combination of cultures and that he does not have to pick one side of the family to follow.

Another cultural conflict is emphasized through the tensions between Antonio's life at home and life at school. At home, Antonio speaks only Spanish and follows the cultural expectations with which he has grown up. When Antonio goes to school, he is forced to experience the English-speaking academic world of the rest of the United States. He must learn to speak English and interact with children who are not from the same culture as he is. Although Antonio's mother is extremely proud of his opportunity to learn English, Antonio finds that his schoolmates are less accepting of his own culture.

Antonio ultimately learns that he is able to accept elements of every culture when he creates his own identity and follows his own path to adulthood. Ultima assures him that not every type of faith is mutually exclusive, and Antonio is able to use the same lesson in dealing with the conflicting cultures in his life.

Good versus Evil

The conflict between good and evil in the novel is characterized through the relationship between Ultima and Tenorio. From the start, Ultima is described as the moral compass for the novel, protecting her community from the curses of evil witches. Tenorio, on the other hand, takes his place as Ultima's arch-nemesis who shares his wicked daughters' penchant for cruelty and evil. The battle between these two characters perpetuates the majority of the plot in the novel and, although both characters die at the end, Ultima's goodness and Tenorio's evilness are maintained.

However, as Antonio himself discovers, good and evil are not so easy to distinguish. Although Ultima performs many good deeds, she kills two of Tenorio's daughters with her counter curse, using pagan powers that go against Catholic beliefs. The incident with the holy cross in Chapter 12 brings to light additional questions about Ultima's "goodness" in the eyes of the church. Tenorio's true evil is equally difficult to determine; his attempts to murder Ultima are only the result of his wish to avenge his daughter's death. In some novels, a mourning father who seeks revenge would be the hero, rather than the antagonist. In both cases, neither character is easy to define as wholly good or wholly evil.

Near the end of the novel, Anaya explains that the goodness of a person is determined solely by his or her actions. Within this framework, Ultima still possesses much more "good" in her nature than Tenorio does. However, it is clear that good and evil cannot be distinguished in a clear-cut way, and this is one of the more important lessons that Antonio learns about life.

Myth

Myth is a very important theme in the novel because it is an underlying presence in the culture that surrounds Antonio. He comes across many different kinds of myths over the course of the book. Some of these come specifically from Native American culture, such as the story of the Golden Carp, while others come from a more general culture of pagan beliefs about the natural world, such as Ultima's views toward plant life. The combination of these myths with Catholicism is a direct result of the colonization of New Mexico by Spanish colonists. As the colonist communities began to blend with the communities of Native Americans, the result was an amalgamation of cultures in which these myths maintained their importance alongside Catholic doctrine.

The myth of the Golden Carp, in particular, outlines a new set of beliefs for Antonio that he had never considered before. Although these beliefs initially seem to conflict with his Catholic upbringing, Antonio grows to realize that the Golden Carp simply offers a different perspective to the world than Catholicism. Neither is better than the other, but a combination of both is the way to find a satisfying faith. In the same way, Ultima's explanation of the spirit in the natural world and the presence of the river allow Antonio to gain a broader scope of understanding.

In the book, Antonio's discovery of these myths helps him to develop his own understanding of faith. By combining the beliefs that he learns from Christianity with the ideas he develops from the Golden Carp and from Ultima, Antonio is able to choose his own path, developing his own identity from all of the religious and cultural ideas available.

Family Expectations

Antonio's relationships with his brothers, his parents, and his uncles are extremely significant throughout the novel. Because Antonio comes from such a tightly-knit family, he feels a great deal of pressure coming from every side when it comes to determining his future. While his mother and his Luna uncles want him to become a farmer priest like their side of the family, his father and Marez uncles want him to become a vaquero like them. Antonio feels an obligation correspond to these desires, but he also wants to follow in the footsteps of his older brothers, all of whom he views in an idealized way. Antonio is especially willing to model himself off of the example of Andrew, and he is hopelessly disappointed to discover that his favorite brother is not actually worthy of such veneration. While Antonio strives to emulate his brothers, his brothers in turn have their own expectations for him. Because they chose to follow the lifestyle of the Marez, they have decided that Antonio must follow the Luna side of the family, simply to maintain the balance and fairness between the two families.

It is only after Ultima arrives that Antonio is able to gain some independence from the obligations he feels in his family. This freedom is largely due to the fact that Ultima is not an actual member of the family: she brings a freeing outside perspective to his future and does not have any ulterior motives when it comes to aiding his development as an individual. With Ultima's help, Antonio is able to extricate himself from the oppressive expectations of his family and make his own decisions about his path in life.

Dreams of the Parents versus Dreams of the Children

Throughout the book, Antonio's father hopes to fulfill his dream of moving to California with his sons. Because he had to give up his vaquero lifestyle to move to Guadalupe, Gabriel views this dream as his last remaining hope for contentment in life. Ever since his sons were children, Antonio's father has expected them to follow his dream as well. When Antonio's brothers return from war, Gabriel believes that the time for his dream is finally at hand, but he is dismayed to discover that his sons have no interest in California and wish to pursue their own dreams. This conflict must come to a breaking point when Leon, Eugene, and eventually Andrew abandon their father's dream in order to move to Las Vegas and seek their fortune.

Similarly, Antonio's mother dreams that Antonio will be a priest to lead her Luna people back to the stability that they had once known. As a woman, Antonio's mother could never hope to take this position herself, and she must see her dreams realized through her youngest son. Moreover, Maria chooses to shape her dream as she sees fit: instead of telling Antonio that the Luna priest was also the father, she creates a holier vision of a priest who remains physically pure. Although Maria's dream is not rejected to the extent that Gabriel's dream is, it still comes into conflict with Antonio's eventual decision to pursue his own dreams. By the end of the novel, we are still unclear as to what path Antonio will follow in life; as a man of learning, he could be a priest to the Lunas or he could be something else. Either way, it is clear that Maria will be forced to acknowledge Antonio's independence at some point later in his life.

In both cases, the children in the Marez family are forced to grow up under the shadow of their parents' dreams. Neither parent intends to oppress their children with their expectations, but both Gabriel and Maria have a difficult time accepting that Antonio and his brothers must lead independent lives.

World War II

Although World War II does not play a large role in the events of the novel, it is extremely significant in the way that it shapes certain characters. As the novel opens, the Marez family is incomplete because Leon, Eugene, and Andrew are all fighting overseas. As a six year old, Antonio does not understand the political issues that perpetuated World War II, but he does recognize the strain that his brothers' absence places on the family. When the brothers return and the family is once more complete, things have still changed from the way that they were. All three men are suffering from post-traumatic stress from their experiences during the war. Because of the horrors that they experienced in the war, none of Antonio's brothers are able to integrate themselves back into the quiet life of Guadalupe; Antonio describes them as "dying giants" because they can no longer cope with the life that they left behind when they went to war. Their decision to leave Guadalupe is indirectly linked to their experiences in the war.

The war also appears indirectly in one of the very first traumatic experiences described in the book: Lupito's death. Like Antonio's brothers, Lupito is also a veteran of the war, and he has a much more severe case of the "war sickness." His war sickness becomes so overwhelming that he murders the sheriff of Guadalupe and ends up with a standoff at the bridge. As Antonio's close observation of Lupito shows, Lupito does not intend to kill any of the men of the bridge; instead of firing at them, he shoots in the air to draw their fire. Lupito is so hopeless from his experiences in the war that he essentially chooses to commit suicide, placing himself in a position to be shot by the men on the bridge. This particular incident is Antonio's first step to discovering the horrors of the world, and because of it, Antonio's innocence is also a victim of the war sickness and World War II.

Glossary of Terms

abrazo
an embrace

absolution
a release from the consquences of a sin

acequia
an irrigation ditch or gutter

adobe
sun-dried bricks made of mud and straw

Agua Negra
a Spanish phrase meaning "black water"

Ah la veca!
a Spanish slang phrase referring to the penis

alfalfa
a small plant with purple flowers, often used as hay for cattle

amigo
a male friend

Arrimense vivos y difuntos, aqui estamos todos juntos
"They approach alive and deceased here we are all together"

atole
a porridge made from cornmeal and milk or water

audacity
boldness, often with an arrogant element

Ay Dios, otro dia!
"Oh God, another day!"

Benas dias te de Dios, a ti y a tu familia

"Good day to God, to you, and to your family"

bile

a yellowish-green liquid used in the process of digestion

bizcochitos

little biscuits

bosque

a grove of cottonwood trees

bruja

a witch who practices black magic

bulto

a bulk or shape

cabrón

a Spanish slang word meaning "bastard" or "cuckold"

cabritos, cabroncitos

kids, or small goats; used in this case as a term of endearment

campana

a church bell

campo santo

burial grounds

catechism

a form of instruction in Catholic doctrine based on the fundamental principles of Christianity

chango

a Spanish term of endearment meaning "little monkey" or "little child"

chicos

dried corn

chile

a type of red pepper used commonly in Southwestern cooking

chingada

a Spanish slang word meaning "sexual intercourse" or "what a nuisance!"

comanchero

an Indian trader

Como te llamas?

"What is your name?"

compadre

an associate or friend

conquistador

a conqueror or an adventurer

contrivance

a scheme or plan

corral

a fenced-in area for horses

crudo

hung over from drinking too much alcohol

cuento

a story based on folklore

cuidado

a Spanish word meaning "care" as in "take care!"

culvert

a drain that crosses under a road

curandera

a female folk healer who uses herbal remedies

desgraciado

a Spanish word meaning "miserable" or "unhappy"

diablo

a devil

diente

a Spanish word meaning "tooth"

disquietude

uneasiness

Donde esta?

"Where is he?"

dulce

sweet

eddie

a small whirlpool

el policia

a policeman

el Rito

the Bito Creek

empanadita

a pastry or turnover filled with ground meat, vegetables, or fruit

En el nombre del Padre, del Hijo, y el Espiritu Santo

"In the name of the Father, the Son, and the Holy Spirit"

encanto

a charm or spell

entremetido

a Spanish word meaning "busybody"

Es una mujer que no ha pecado

"It is a woman who has not sinned"

Es verdad

"It is true"

Espiritu de mi alma

"Spirit of my soul"

Esta sola, ya no queda gente en el pueblito de Las Pasturas

"She is alone, there are not people in the village of Las Pasturas"

farol

a lantern

gabacha

a white woman

Gracias a Dios que venites

"Thanks to God who comes"

Gracias por mi vida

Thank you for my life

grillo

a cricket

hechicera

a Spanish word meaning "enchantress"

heresy

a belief that is contrary to accepted religious doctrine

hermano

a Spanish word meaning "brother"

hi-jo-la

a reference to "hijo de la chingada," which means "son of the screwed one"

hijo

a Spanish word meaning "son"

hombre

a Spanish word meaning "a man"

huevos

balls or testicles

iglesia

a Spanish word meaning "church"

Jason no esta aqui

"Jason is not here"

jodido

a Spanish slang word meaning "shitty"

kerosene

a type of thin oil used as fuel for heat or cooking

la llorona

"the crying woman"; in New Mexican folklore, the ghost of a woman who is weeping for her drowned children

la muerte

a Spanish word meaning "death"

la tristesa de la vida

a Spanish phrase meaning "the sadness of life"

las putas

a Spanish slang phrase meaning "the whores"

lazo

a long rope with a loop, used for catching horses and cattle

llama

a Spanish word meaning "flame"

llano

an open plain with few trees; common in the Southwestern United States

Lo mató!

"He killed him!"

Madre de Dios

a Spanish phrase meaning "Mother of God"

maiz

Indian corn

maldito

a Spanish word meaning "cursed"

manta

shawl

manzanilla

chamomile, a type of plant with medicinal purposes, often used to make tea

melancholy

depressed or gloomy

mesquite bush

a type of tree or shrub common to New Mexico; characterized by spiny leaves and resistance to drought

mira

a Spanish word meaning "Look!"

mitote

a riot or an uproar

molino

a mill

mollera

the top of the head

monotonous

boring or tedious

muchacho

a Spanish word meaning "boy" or "chap"

mujer

a Spanish word meaning "a woman"

muy sabrosos

a Spanish phrase meaning "very tasty"

nopal

a prickly pear from a cactus

novena

a series of Catholic prayers that take place over the course of nine days

ominous

dark foreshadowing or foreboding

oregano

a type of herb used in cooking; also used by Ultima to cure cough and fever

oshá

a medicinal plant

partitioned

divided into parts

Pase, Grande, pase. Nuestra casa es su casa

"Come in, Grande. Our house is your house"

penance

a punishment undergone to show sorrow for a sin or wrong-doing

perdón

a Spanish word meaning "I'm sorry"

Pero qué dices?

"What are you saying?"

pesadilla

a nightmare

pinon

a type of pine tree common in the Southwestern United States

Por la sangre de Lupito, todos debemos de rogar, que Dioes la saque de pena y la lleve a descansar

"For the blood of Lupito, all must pray that God remove the sorrow and take him to rest"

posole

a thick hominy stew with pork or chicken, chile peppers, and coriander

precarious

unstable or insecure

puto

a Spanish slang word meaning "a male prostitute"

Que Dios te bendiga

"May God bless you"

Que pasa aqui?

"What is going on here?

Que pasa?

What happened?

que suerte

a Spanish phrase meaning "what luck!"

Quien es?

"Who is it?"

ranchero

a rancher

ristra

a rope, usually made from chile

sala

a living room

sangre

a Spanish word meaning "blood"

satchel

a small bag

scapular

a small object made up of two squares of cloth attached to one another; worn underneath the clothes, the devotional scapular is said to provide spiritual benefit to the wearer

shellack

a thin varnish

spectral

ghostly

stupor

a daze

Te voy a matar, cabron!

"I am going to kill you, goat!"

tejano

a native of Texas

tenacious

to be persistent and stubborn

tio

a Spanish word meaning "uncle"

tortilla

a thin pancake made from cornmeal or wheat flour

treacherous

dangerous; also untrustworthy

tripas

intestines

turgid

swollen or distended

un momento

a Spanish phrase meaning "one moment"

Una mujer con un deinte, que llama a toda la gente

"A woman with a tooth, who calls all the people"

vagabond

an unsettled nomad who wanders from place to place

vaquero

a cowboy

velorio

a wake for the dead

ven aca

a Spanish phrase meaning "come here"

vieja

a Spanish word meaning "an old woman"

Voy a tirar tripas!

"I am going to throw up!"

war sickness

post-traumatic stress or trauma related to war

Y las companas de la iglesia estan doblando

"And the church bells were tolling"

Ya vengo

"I'm coming"

yucca

a type of plant with sword-shaped leaves and white flowers; the yucca flower is the state flower of New Mexico

Short Summary

Bless Me, Ultima is a coming-of-age story centered on a Mexican-American boy named Antonio Marez and his family in New Mexico in the mid-1940s. The novel opens when Ultima, a curandera or folk healer, comes to live with Antonio's family. Antonio is only six years old when the novel begins, but he is already anxious about what the future holds for him. His mother is a Luna, from a family of devoutly Catholic farmers, while his father is a Marez, from a family of wild vaqueros, or cowboys, that roam the llano. Antonio feels the pressure of expectation from both of these families, and he is unsure of how he can reconcile the two cultures in his own life.

When Ultima joins the Marez household, Antonio views her as a figure of wisdom and guidance and relies upon her judgment in determining the course of his life. He discovers that Ultima was present at his birth and thus is the only person who knows whether Antonio will follow the Luna or the Marez way of life. Ultima introduces Antonio to her beliefs about the natural world, taking him on long walks along the river and teaching him the names and functions of the herbs that she uses. It is when he is with Ultima that Antonio first senses the presence of the river, a spirit of harmony in the natural world.

One day, the peace of the household is shattered when Chavez rushes to the house to tell Antonio's father that the sheriff has been murdered by Lupito, a war veteran suffering from the "war sickness." Antonio's father joins Chavez and the other men of the town to find and kill Lupito before he can do any more harm. Antonio secretly follows them and, inadvertently crossing paths with Lupito along the banks of the river, witnesses Lupito's violent death at the hands of the mob. This moment of Lupito's death marks the first step in Antonio's loss of innocence and also spurs his preoccupation with sin, punishment, and morality.

When the fall arrives, Antonio begins to go to school. Although he is anxious at the prospect of being separated from his mother, he is fascinated by the "magic of letters" and wants to learn how to use their power for himself. Antonio's mother continues to pressure him to become a priest and begs Ultima to tell her of her son's future. Ultima replies that Antonio will be a man of learning. Antonio excels at school, but he begins to experience a cultural conflict for the first time when the white children at school taunt him for speaking Spanish and for eating Mexican food.

World War II ends and Antonio's three soldier brothers are sent home to rejoin the family. Gabriel is thrilled that his three oldest sons are returning home, and he hopes finally to fulfill his lifelong dream of moving to California. When Leon, Eugene, and Andrew arrive home, however, they are traumatized by their experiences in the war and are unable to adjust back to the quiet life of Guadalupe. They are equally unwilling to accompany their father in his dream of California and wish to pursue their own independent lives. After a fight with their father, Leon and Eugene move to Las Vegas, leaving Andrew behind. Antonio does not understand the conflict between his brothers and his father or the way that they are able to reject the expectations of their family. Still preoccupied with his questions of sin and punishment, Antonio begins to express anxiety about his brothers and their seeming loss of innocence. Antonio's mother assures him that he will understand everything when he takes his first Communion, and Antonio looks forward to this moment of epiphany.

One day, Antonio goes fishing with Samuel, a friend from school, and tells him of his questions about God and judgment. Samuel replies by telling Antonio the story of the golden carp, a pagan deity that protects mankind and maintains the harmony of the natural world. Antonio is uncertain of how to reconcile this new religious information with his Catholic upbringing, but he is still intrigued by the possibilities that the golden carp reveals. Antonio's questions about Catholicism are heightened when his uncle Lucas is cursed by the witch-like Trementina sisters. Despite the best efforts of a priest, Lucas' condition continues to deteriorate, and he is only cured when Ultima steps in. Antonio realizes that Ultima's power cannot be explained by the Catholic Church, and he does not know how to deal with the possibility of conflicting beliefs.

In the summer, Cico takes Antonio to visit the garden of Narciso. Narciso is known as the town drunk, but Antonio is amazed to see the lush garden that he has created. He realizes that Narciso is one figure in which the conflicting backgrounds of Luna and Marez are balanced: Narciso lives as a vaquero on the llano, but he also has a close connection to the earth and cycle of life. Antonio also begins to understand the prejudices that inform peoples' actions and beliefs, even when they are unjust.

Cico takes Antonio to see the golden carp and tells him of the apocalypse that the golden carp has prophesied. He explains that the land is full of sinners, and the golden carp will flood the land in order to purge it of sin and rebuild it in purity. Antonio is horrified at this prophesy and does not understand why everyone must be destroyed for the sins of a few people. Cico replies that every person sins. Faced with the prospect of a harsh Christian god and an equally harsh pagan god, Antonio wishes that there were a god who was forgiving and compassionate.

In winter, a massive blizzard strikes the town of Guadalupe. Antonio goes to school anyway to take part in the Christmas play and, as he is returning home, he witnesses a violent fight between Narciso and Tenorio. Tenorio, the father of the Trementina sisters, is mourning the death of his first daughter and is determined to revenge himself upon Ultima. Badly injured, Narciso tries to get Andrew to help him protect Ultima, but Andrew is distracted by his girl at Rosie's brothel and refuses to help. Narciso decides to warn Ultima himself and begins the trek up to Antonio's house while Antonio secretly follows. On his way, Tenorio ambushes Narciso and kills him, forcing Antonio to witness another violent death at a very young age. Antonio develops a high fever and suffers from terrible nightmares for the next several days. When Antonio recovers, he finds out that Tenorio has been cleared of any blame for

Narciso's death; the town coroner has decided that Narciso died an accidental death due to his drinking. Antonio is again exposed to the fact that prejudice can interfere with justice.

When spring arrives, it is finally time for Antonio to take his first Communion. He takes lessons in catechism from Father Byrnes for several weeks and still hopes that his first Communion will be the moment when he finally understands God and receives the answers to his questions. Yet Antonio's faith is also confused by the differing beliefs of the people around him. Both Ultima and Antonio's father are Christians but seem to worship the natural world more than religious doctrine. Florence, one of Antonio's friends, goes so far as to declare his atheism and constantly directs Antonio to notice the inherent failings of Christianity. When Antonio receives his first Communion, he waits expectantly to hear God's voice but is dismayed to hear only silence. His faith is seriously damaged, and Antonio wonders if God is dead or if He ever existed. He still does not understand why there is evil in the world that remains unpunished.

As the months pass, Antonio grows closer to Ultima, even to the point that he feels more connected to her than he does to his mother. She continues to impart her wisdom about the world to him, and Antonio begins to realize the importance of moral independence. Antonio and his father help Antonio to dispel a curse on a local house, and Antonio is again fascinated by the failure of the Catholic priest where Ultima succeeds. One day, Antonio visits the golden carp and decides to teach the story to Florence; he hopes that he will be able to give Florence some hope in his life. Before he can tell Florence about the golden carp, however, Florence drowns in the river.

Extremely traumatized by his witnessing of this third death, Antonio is sent to work on the Luna farm for the summer. Ultima hopes that the distance from Guadalupe will help Antonio cope with his grief in a better way. During the journey to the farm, Antonio's father tells him that the way of the vaquero is ended and that Antonio should choose his own destiny by selecting the best qualities of the Lunas and the Marez to uses as his own. Antonio spends several happy weeks at the Luna farm. As he works with his uncles and grandfather, Antonio begins to understand his mother's people and appreciate their silence and connection to the earth. Although he still does not know if he will follow the path of a Luna and become a priest, he feels that he could be happy in the lifestyle.

During his stay with the Lunas, Antonio hears that Tenorio's second daughter has died and Tenorio is determined to kill Ultima once and for all. He is ambushed and nearly trampled to death by Tenorio near his grandfather's farm, and Tenorio taunts Antonio with the knowledge that Ultima's life is linked to the life of her owl. Realizing that Tenorio plans to murder Ultima's owl to kill her, Antonio runs back to Guadalupe to warn her. He is too late and arrives just in time to see Tenorio shoot the owl. Before Tenorio can murder Antonio as well, Antonio's uncle Pedro kills Tenorio. Because the owl is Ultima's spirit, she must die as well, but she comforts

Antonio by explaining that her death will restore the natural harmony of the world. She gives Antonio a final blessing and, at her request, Antonio buries the owl beneath a forked juniper tree in the hills.

Summary and Analysis of Chapter 1 (Uno)

The novel opens with the adult Antonio Marez describing the events that occurred when he was six years old. For Antonio, his development begins not with his birth or with his first days of school, but with the arrival of Ultima, the curandera who moves in with his family the summer before his seventh birthday. It is with Ultima's arrival that Antonio is first exposed to the magic of the world and the beauty and power of the llano.

The night before Ultima is due to arrive, Antonio lies awake in bed, listening to his parents talk about Ultima. Both of his parents speak of her with a great deal of reverence and awe. Antonio's father respects her because she has been an important figure in his home village of Las Pasturas and shares his love of the llano. Antonio's mother is even more attached to her because Ultima helped her in childbirth and was her companion during her lonely years on the llano. Antonio's mother is concerned that Ultima must live alone on the llano during her old age and urges her husband to bring the curandera to live with them.

She is particularly empathetic to Ultima's life on the llano because she was born to farmers and was not happy in the world of the vaqueros to which her husband belongs. While Gabriel Marez was happy as a cowboy, living off of the land, Antonio's mother missed the religion and stability of town and the farm. Eventually Maria convinced Gabriel to move to the town of Guadalupe for the sake of their children's education, but Gabriel still has not adjusted to the new life and misses his days as a vaquero. Although Maria is happy, Gabriel has lost the respect of his former compadres and spends his weekends drinking and dreaming of a free life in California.

After Maria and Gabriel argue briefly about their former days on the llano (Maria emphasizes that they were "hard days," and Gabriel responds that they were "good days"), Gabriel informs his wife that he has already sent word for Ultima to leave the llano and come to live with their family. Gabriel is concerned about Ultima's influence on the children because of her power to lift curses and knowledge of herbs and plants and ancient magic, but Maria alleviates his fear.

Antonio is intrigued by these brief descriptions of Ultima and, falling asleep, immediately begins to dream about his birth at Ultima's hands. In his dream, Antonio sees himself drawn out from his mother by Ultima and then observes as the conflict sides of his family argue over his destiny. The Lunas, the family of Antonio's mother, wish Antonio to become a priest and a farmer. His uncles and grandfather mark his forehead with earth so that he will be connected to the ground. The Marez vaqueros, the family of Antonio's father, barge in and immediately refute the Lunas' claim on Antonio. Antonio, they argue, will be a vaquero who wanders the llano on horseback. The tensions between the two families begin to heighten until

Ultima asserts that only she will know Antonio's destiny and path for life.

Antonio awakes from this dream with the sound of his father's truck and desperately wants to see Ultima and the village of Las Pasturas for himself. Although he tries to dress quickly, he is unable to catch the truck before his father leaves, and he must wait patiently for Ultima to arrive. As he is surveying the landscape, Antonio notices the schoolhouse near the church and immediately voices anxiety about going to school in the fall. To rid himself of his anxieties, Antonio swiftly completes his chores and then eats a breakfast of atole and tortillas with his mother and two sisters, Theresa and Deborah.

Maria Marez coaches Antonio and his two sisters on the proper way to address Ultima when she arrives. She must be addressed as La Grande, Antonio's mother asserts, and then reminds her children of the great honor that they should feel at sharing house with such an esteemed figure. As Maria prepares for Ultima's arrival, Antonio asks her about the circumstances of his birth, wondering if his dream was a reflection of reality. Maria confirms the truth of Antonio's dream, acknowledging that the Lunas and the Marez fought ferociously over Antonio's destiny until Ultima took charge. As Maria begins to enumerate of the many negative qualities of the Marez, Antonio reflects on the fact that his dream was reality and becomes even more anxious to meet Ultima face-to-face.

While he waits, Antonio runs to see if his friend Jason is home. He is not: his mother sadly explains in Spanish that Jason is visiting his Indian, a figure of whom Jason's father severely disapproves. Disappointed, Antonio returns home, and shortly later, Ultima arrives. Theresa and Deborah make their introductions exactly as Antonio's mother had requested, saying clearly, "Buenos dias le de Dios, Grande." When Antonio faces Ultima, however, he is transfixed by her eyes and feels the power of a whirlwind wash around him when he takes her hand. Unable to say his mother's coached introduction, he calls Ultima by her first name. Antonio's mother tries to chide him, but Ultima quickly intercedes, explaining that she has a special bond with Antonio because he is the last of the Marez children that she helped to birth.

Antonio also notices that Ultima is accompanied by an owl that sits near the house. Although Deborah and Theresa are frightened of the owl, Antonio is strangely comforted by its presence and dreams of the Virgin of Guadalupe being lifted into heaven by the owl.

Analysis:

This opening chapter immediately sets up one of the main conflicts of the novel: the conflict between the Luna family and the Marez family. While Antonio's mother desperately wants him to follow in the footsteps of his Luna ancestors and become a priest, Antonio's father would prefer that he becomes a vaquero and lead a free life on the llano. Antonio's anxiety and resistance to change is demonstrated by his nervousness at attending school in the upcoming months. Not only does he not wish to be separated from his mother, he is anxious about what the future holds for him and what destiny he is expected to pursue.

This conflict is characterized in Antonio's dream where he actually sees the two sides of his family fighting over his destiny. Even though Antonio is only six years old, he already feels the pressure of these conflicting desires and does not know how to deal with both familial expectations. The schism between his own desires and that of the family for him foreshadows a battle that will plague him all his life. The only comfort to Antonio is Ultima's presence at his birth and her declaration that she is the only person who will truly know Antonio's future path. As such, Antonio looks forward to her arrival at their house because of the insight that she might give him into his future.

This chapter also outlines the first introduction of Ultima as a significant character in the novel and the dichotomy that exists between pagan beliefs and Catholicism. In New Mexican culture, Christianity is tied closely to the pagan beliefs and myths that defined the native communities before the arrival of the Spanish colonists. Although Ultima is a curandera with the knowledge of herbs and plants, she is also a Catholic who adheres to Catholic holidays and expectations. Yet, her Catholicism does not overshadow or even necessarily equal the scope of her other power, a fact which is highlighted in the mob scene at the end of Chapter 12.

Both of Antonio's parents respect Ultima, but Antonio's father is still wary of her position as a curandera and the power that is said to go with it. His concern that she might have a negative influence on their children goes hand-in-hand with his appreciation for her from the perspective of a vaquero. Antonio's mother, on the other hand, is devoutly Catholic, but chooses to overlook the pagan elements of Ultima's life to view her as a close friend. In both cases, Christianity and pagan beliefs are not mutually exclusive but somehow coexist in the culture of Guadalupe.

Antonio's immediate trust of Ultima also demonstrates this uneasy balance. If Ultima were evil or an antagonist against Catholicism, Antonio would not be able to feel so comfortable in her presence. Moreover, even though he knows that owls are usually the symbol of a bruja, or witch, Antonio somehow senses that Ultima's owl is different. Although religion cannot explain Ultima's powers, Antonio and his family are still able to acknowledge and embrace her as both a curandera and a Catholic.

Summary and Analysis of Chapters 2-3 (Dos-Tres)

The second chapter opens with Antonio's description of Ultima's easy adaptation to the daily life in the Marez household. Antonio's mother is happy to have another woman to talk to and no longer feels lonely on their isolated land. Antonio's sisters are pleased with Ultima because her help around the house means that they are not required to do as many household chores. Even Antonio's father is pleased to have Ultima living in their house because he has another person to talk to about his dream of moving to California with his sons. Antonio is also happy with Ultima's presence because she takes him on long walks along the riverbanks and teaches him about plant life, local animals, and the spirit of the river.

On Saturday night, the peace is interrupted by Chavez, who runs to the house and urges Antonio's father to accompany him to the bridge. The sheriff, his brother, Chavez exclaims, has been murdered by Lupito, a townsman who has been suffering from the war sickness since his time fighting in World War II. All of the men of the town are assembling at the bridge in order to hunt down Lupito and ensure that he does not kill anyone else. Antonio's father tells Maria to lock all of the doors and then seizes a rifle and walks to the bridge with Chavez, unaware that Antonio is secretly following them.

In order to make sure that his father does not notice him, Antonio takes a different route along the river and inadvertently comes across Lupito, who is hiding in the reeds a few yards away. Antonio watches as Lupito is momentarily sighted by the men on the bridge and then lost again in the darkness. The men on the bridge begin to argue about killing Lupito; some argue that he is an animal that must be shot, while Antonio's father and Narciso, the town drunk, urge the men to be respectful of life. Narciso tries to talk to Lupito from the bridge, reminding him that they are friends and that he understands the war sickness. Antonio watches as Lupito reacts physically to Narciso's voice and seems to be about to turn himself in but then shoots his pistol into the air to draw their fire.

At the sound of the gunshots, the men on the bridge immediately shoot in their direction and swiftly kill Lupito. Shocked by what he has just witnessed, Antonio immediately begins to run home, praying the Act of Contrition to himself over and over again. As Antonio is about to despair, he hears the gentle hooting of Ultima's owl and is comforted enough to reach his house. Before he can enter his room, though, Ultima intercepts him and, recognizing what he has just witnessed, brings him into her room to treat his cuts. Warm in Ultima's bed and hearing the comforting sound of the owl outside, Antonio is eased into sleep and begins to dream about his three brothers, off fighting at war.

In his dream, Antonio's three brothers argue about their destinies as men of the llano, certain to wander forever in response to their wild Marez blood. Antonio urges his brothers to join with him in accompanying their father on his dream to California, but they laugh at him, asserting that Antonio must be a man of the Lunas for the sake of their mother. Antonio tries to follow their brothers as they cross the river, but he begins to hear a tormented sound along the river. Fearfully, his brothers first declare that the wailing is la llorona and then determine that it is the soul of Lupito trying to take Antonio. Antonio declares that it is neither, but rather the presence of the river.

At the beginning of the third chapter, Antonio wakes up amazed that his cuts from the night before are almost gone. This must be a testament to Ultima's skill with medicinal herbs. Although he feels better than he did immediately after watching Lupito die, Antonio is now preoccupied with questions of sin and morality, wondering what has become of Lupito's soul. Will he go to Hell because he is a murderer, or will God forgive him of his sins and allow him to go to Purgatory? Or will he become a ghost that haunts people along the river?

As he lies in bed thinking, Antonio hears his mother calling his father to wake up and waits for the inevitable argument that always happens between his parents on Sunday mornings. Antonio's father does not share his wife's religious inclinations and usually spends his Sundays recovering from a hangover from his Saturday-night drinking. When he is drunk, he pokes fun at the priests and his wife's religion and then bemoans the fact that he sacrificed his life on the llano for the daughter of a farmer. Antonio's mother always counters by arguing that the Marez are stubborn freethinkers and blasphemers. She refers to the first priest who came to El Puerto, the land of her family, and settled the land while giving faith and religion to the people. This is the destiny that she would choose for Antonio: a priest who rules over a community of farmers.

When Antonio gets up and goes downstairs his mother urges him and his sisters to pray for departed souls when they go to church. This reminder of the events of the previous night sparks Antonio's questions and anxieties about Lupito's fate once again, but he is calmed by Ultima's presence. Before they leave for church, Antonio's mother and father begin to argue about Antonio's future again. Antonio's mother, in particular, wishes that Antonio could always keep his innocence. The only way that he can do this, she asserts, is if he is always with God and becomes a priest. Antonio's father is exasperated and ends the argument by declaring that Antonio will decide his own fate when the time comes.

Antonio quickly performs his chores, feeding the rabbits and letting out the cow, all the while trying not to think of Lupito's murder. He runs back to the house for a quick hair-combing, and then the family leaves for mass. While they walk, Ultima's presence is observed anxiously by the other families in the neighborhood. Ultima walks over to Antonio, and Antonio asks her how his father can take communion after killing a man. Ultima comforts Antonio by assuring him that his father did not shoot Lupito; a man of the llano is always very respectful of life. On the path to the church, Antonio notices Rosie's brothel, which rests slightly off of Main Street.

                              Summary and Analysis of Chapters 2-3 (Dos-Tres)

As they come closer to the church, the church bell begins to toll a mourning knell for Lupito. Antonio separates from his parents and goes over to the side of the church to talk to the other boys his age. Horse, Ernie, Abel, the Vitamin Kid, Florence, and Samuel are all talking about Lupito's murder. Horse, the biggest member of the gang, notices Antonio and tells him to come closer to wrestle. Although he does not want to wrestle, Antonio walks to Horse and successful flips him on his back. The other boys are nervous about Horse's defeat at the hands of a much younger boy, but Horse laughs it off, and all of the boys run into the church in time for mass.

Analysis:

At the beginning of Chapter 2, we see Antonio beginning to develop as an inquisitive individual under Ultima's influence. Not only is he able to acknowledge the beauty of the natural world around him, but he is able to sense the presence of the river as a benevolent force of nature. This early understanding of the balance and beauty in the world foreshadows the wisdom that Antonio will ultimately gain with Ultima's help.

Antonio's witnessing of Lupito's death is a major crossroads for him as a character. It is his first experience with death, and Antonio is seriously traumatized, both by Lupito's violent end and by the presence of his father among the shooting men. When he runs home, he repeats the Act of Contrition over and over again, even though he doesn't know what it means. Antonio's use of a religious prayer in quest for comfort demonstrates his desires to use religion to explain and fix the problems he observes in life.

Ultimately, Antonio does not receive any comfort from the use of this prayer. He only recites it as a result of his mother's Catholic upbringing, not because he has chosen his faith. Instead, Antonio is comforted when he hears the hooting of Ultima's owl; in fact, it is only after he hears the owl that he is able to think rationally and make his way home. This instance highlights the conflict between Catholicism and paganism as Antonio begins on the search for his own faith.

After witnessing the murder, Antonio becomes preoccupied with Lupito's fate and questions of sin and punishment. He does not know how to reconcile Lupito's madness and death with Catholic ideas of God. Although Lupito's actions as a murderer make him doomed to Hell, Antonio realizes that his actions were caused by his war sickness, and Lupito cannot be blamed for what happened. Yet, he knows that the God of Christianity is not forgiving or compassionate and thus, not likely to release Lupito from the horrors of Hell. Moreover, although Lupito murdered the sheriff, the men of the town also murdered him. Will they not be punished for murder as well? For the first time, Antonio is unable to reconcile what he knows is right with the expectations of his religion.

In his second dream of the novel, Antonio reiterates his anxieties about his future and his family. His three brothers have already determined their Marez blood and will spend their lives wandering. Antonio wants to keep the family together and support his father, but his brothers insist that he becomes a priest to make his mother happy. Again, Antonio is torn between two parents and two paths. His religious ambivalence is also highlighted in this dream when Antonio identifies the wailing in the river as first, la Llorona, a mythical figure from New Mexican folklore, and then, as Lupito's soul. However, Antonio accepts neither the pagan explanation nor the Catholic explanation as the truth. Instead, he determines that the wailing is the presence of the river, neither Catholic nor pagan, but simply an element of nature.

In chapter 3, Antonio continues his preoccupation with sin and punishment but is guided on his exploration by Ultima. Ultima tries to explain to Antonio that the men of the llano, like his father, would never kill without just cause; this is the characteristic that distinguishes their murder of Lupito from his murder of the sheriff. Ultima also explains that people must make their own moral decisions, regardless of whether or not they correspond to religious framework. Although Antonio thinks about what Ultima has said, he is still unable to comprehend a world in which morality is separate from Catholic doctrine. Antonio's confusion is not helped by his mother's definition of growing up. Instead of a necessary part of life and development, Antonio's mother believes that the passage into adulthood is dependent on an acceptance of sin. The only way to grow up, she argues, is to be sinful and thus, only if Antonio becomes a priest will he be able to enter adulthood with his innocence. Antonio's father takes a more rational approach, arguing that growing up is a part of life and not something to be dreaded. He believes that a person's experiences in life define who he or she is as an individual and create the layers of a person's character.

It is at this point that we first see the extent to which Antonio feels pressure to be a priest. No matter what his father says, Antonio believes that sin and adulthood are closely related. Not only must he follow the expectations of his Luna family by becoming a priest, but he must do so simply to avoid being corrupted with sin. This explanation of the relationship between sin and adulthood contributes to Antonio's general fear of sin, and his desire to avoid losing his innocence at all costs. Ironically, Antonio's mother makes this claim after Antonio has witnessed Lupito's murder and perhaps already lost his innocence forever.

                    Summary and Analysis of Chapters 2-3 (Dos-Tres)

Summary and Analysis of Chapters 4-7 (Cuatro-Siete)

As the summer comes to a close, Antonio spends most of his time with Ultima. During their daily walks, Ultima introduces him to the plants and herbs that she uses in her medicines, and she explains to Antonio that plants have their own spirits and must be respected. As he observes Ultima walking among the hills, Antonio is deeply impressed by her wisdom and nobility. Later along their walk, Antonio asks Ultima to explain why his father's family is so different from his mother's family. Ultima asserts that the differences in the family have to do with their blood: it is in the blood of the Lunas to be quiet like the moon, and it is in the blood of the Lunas to be wild like the ocean. Considering the contrasts in his family, Antonio wonders which type of life he will choose to live, and he and Ultima fall into silence. During this pause, Antonio becomes first aware of the presence of the river. At first he is frightened, but Ultima calms him and releases him from any further fear of the river.

At home, Antonio helps Ultima to dry the herbs they have gathered by placing them on the roof of the chicken shed. He then eats lunch with his family and spends the rest of the afternoon playing with Jason. After evening, Antonio and his family pray to a beautiful statue of the Virgin of Guadalupe, something that they do every night after supper. The Virgin is Antonio's favorite Saint because of her beauty and forgiving nature. As they are praying to the Virgin of Guadalupe, Antonio begins to wonder again about Lupito's fate. That night, Antonio dreams that his mother asks the Virgin to allow his three older brothers to return home safely and to make Antonio a priest. The Virgin promises that Antonio's older brothers will return safely, but then appears in a dress of mourning for the fourth son, Antonio. Antonio screams in his sleep from the nightmare, but he feels Ultima's hand on his forehead and is able to sleep peacefully.

The next morning, Antonio wakes up to discover that his uncle Pedro is at the house. Uncle Pedro is his favorite of all of his Luna uncles because he is easy to talk to. Antonio and his family load up the truck and drive to El Puerto de los Lunas to help with the harvest. Antonio's family always helps with the summer harvest at the Luna farm, and the trip is the main trip that they take all year. As soon as they arrive, they immediately greet Antonio's grandfather, Prudencio. He is a very wise old man, and he urges Antonio's mother to take faith in God whenever she worries about her sons at war. After the visit, Antonio and his family settle at the home of Juan Lunas, another of Antonio's uncles. While they are working at the harvest, Antonio overhears his uncles talking about him as their one remaining hope for a priest in the family. They decide to invite Antonio to stay with them for a summer to see if he can learn the ways of the Luna.

In the fall, Antonio starts going to school for the first time. He is extremely nervous on his first day, but his parents argue with each other instead of quelling his fears. Antonio's father reiterates that Antonio has Marez blood, while Antonio's mother continues to declare fiercely that he will follow his Luna ancestry. She reminds her husband that, when Antonio was a baby and Ultima offered him all of the objects of life, he reached for the pen and paper. Before Antonio leaves, his mother asks Ultima to tell her what Antonio will be when he grows up. Ultima replies sadly that Antonio will be a man of learning. Triumphantly, Antonio's mother quickly pushes him out the door and on his way to school. As Antonio leaves his house, he feels as if he is seeing Ultima and his parents the way they are for the last time.

Once he reaches the schoolyard, Antonio finds his way to the first grade classroom with some difficulty. Miss Maestas, the first grade teacher, is very nice to Antonio and sets about immediately teaching him how to write. Antonio is intrigued by the magic of letters and works so hard that he is able to write his name by lunchtime. Then, Miss Maestas brings him to the front of the room and introduces him in English to the rest of the class, but the other children laugh at him. Antonio feels even more isolated when he takes out his lunch and notices that all of the other children have sandwiches instead of his beans and tortillas. Ashamed, Antonio sneaks his lunch to the back of the school building and eats silently with George and Willy, two other boys from his town who can share with his sadness and isolation.

At the beginning of Chapter 7, the war has finally ended. All of the teachers at Antonio's school are very happy, but none of the other children seem to be particularly excited. Only Antonio is happy because he knows that the end of the war means that his three older brothers will finally be returning home. Antonio's mother is very excited and joyous that her sons are returning home safely and sets the family at prayer for the evening. They pray for such a long time that Antonio and his sisters fall asleep.

While he is asleep, Antonio dreams that he hears the voices of his brothers calling to him by the river. He cannot see them but he hears their voices and tries to find them. Antonio turns in his dream and discovers three looming shapes behind him and, awakening with a start, runs outside to greet his three brothers who have just come over the crest of the hill next to their house. Antonio's mother cries for a long time, and Antonio's father opens a bottle of whiskey to celebrate, happily reminding his sons that they can now start thinking about moving to California.

Analysis:

In these chapters, Antonio is still extremely preoccupied with Lupito's death and his questions of sin and punishment. The Virgin of Guadalupe is his favorite saint because he associates her with forgiveness and purity. Yet, Antonio is unable to understand how the Virgin could coexist with God if she always forgives sinners and He always punishes sinners. When Antonio dreams of the Virgin wearing mourning for him, he is expressing his own fear that he is sinful instead of good. Indeed, Antonio, as a child, embraces the literalism of religion, finding himself trapped in its inherent contradictions, while still attempting to be faithful to it. Anaya's tone here is neither judgmental nor satiric - simply reflective of a young child's exploratory

   Summary and Analysis of Chapters 4-7 (Cuatro-Siete)

confusion.

At this point in the novel, Antonio also begins to develop a spiritual relationship with the plants and herbs through Ultima's help. His relationship with her strengthens, and he begins to strive to imitate her walk and wisdom. Not only does Ultima teach Antonio about the local plant life, but she introduces him to the cultures and beliefs that defined earlier people, such as the Aztecs and the Moors. Ultima is trying to help Antonio to become grounded in his past and other cultures in an effort to help him forge his own identity. Only if this identity is strong will he be able to survive the gulf in expectations between his own innate desires and those of his family for him.

When Antonio goes to El Puerto to help with the Luna harvest, however, he is immediately thrust back into the pressure of the expectations of his family. His Luna uncles describe him as the one last hope for a priest in their family, and Antonio cannot help but feel the obligation to follow their path. Since his brothers have proven to be too Marez in blood to be a Luna, Antonio is expected to make up for their shortcomings; in other words, the Lunas feel that they are owed one of Maria's sons and, since the elder three have resisted, Antonio is the only remaining possibility for them. This conflict also highlights Antonio's understanding that his brothers may have already lost of innocence when his Luna uncles assert that Antonio is the only brother not yet "lost."

On Antonio's first day of school, Antonio's mother finally receives the evidence that she needs to fulfill her dream that Antonio will be a priest when Ultima admits that Antonio will be a man of learning. However, Ultima does not necessarily mean that Antonio will be a priest. Over the course of the novel, both she and Antonio's father make the claim that individual's learn and grow from their life experiences. With that in mind, every person becomes a "man of learning" if he or she grows from their experiences. Ultima's sadness at this fact could relate to the particular life experiences that are teaching Antonio. Instead of warm and happy life experiences, Antonio is being exposed to death and sadness; paradoxically, becoming a man of learning means that he must be exposed to the harshness of life.

The ending of the war is extremely significant for Antonio and his parents because it means that the entire family will finally be reunited again. In his dream, Antonio sees his brothers as giant figures who ask for his "saving hand." Antonio is clearly unwilling to give up his idealized vision of his brothers, even with the suggestion that they have already lost their innocence. The fact that the giants are "dying" demonstrates that Antonio's effort to maintain this vision of his brothers will be unsuccessful. It also suggests that his brothers will be unable to come back to their old lives in Guadalupe; the war has changed them too much, and they must move on in order to stay alive.

Summary and Analysis of Chapters 8-10 (Ocho-Diez)

The winter passes with the family all together, but Antonio senses that his brothers are beginning to feel restless. They spend the winter months in lethargic states, sleeping during the day and gambling at the pool hall at night. All of them are suffering from post-traumatic stress from their experiences in the war, and Leon, in particular, seems to be the most affected by the war sickness. Throughout the winter, Antonio's father continues to bring up the possibility of moving to California, but none of Antonio's brothers are responsive to the idea.

Once spring arrives, two of Antonio's brothers, Leon and Eugene, decide that they can no longer stay in Guadalupe. They do not want to move to California with their father, but they also do not want to stay in Guadalupe and work on a highway for the rest of their lives. Andrew, the third brother, is more thoughtful and worries about how their parents will react to this decision. Yet, all three of them realize that their father's dream of moving to California is impossible. Their mother's dream, on the other hand, is still a possibility; Antonio can still become a priest for the Lunas. Antonio offers to bless his brothers before they leave, but they laugh at him and, after giving him a quick spanking, toss him on top of the chicken coop. As he sees his brothers walking down the hill in the direction of Rosie's brothel, Antonio feels a great sadness and wishes that he could give them a true blessing.

That night, Antonio has another dream. His brothers lead him to Rosie's brothel and beckon for him to enter with them. Antonio refuses to enter; if he is to be a priest, he must remain innocent of these sins. Antonio begs his brothers not to enter the house of sin, but Eugene and Leon both ignore him and enter. Andrew laughs at Antonio and promises that he will not enter until Antonio has lost his innocence. Antonio hears the voices of his mother and the priest exclaiming that innocence disappears with knowledge. Accompanied by a bolt of lightning, the figure of Ultima appears in the dream and declares that Antonio's innocence lies in the lonely winds of the llano.

Antonio wakes from his dream to discover that his brothers are shouting at his parents downstairs. Leon and Eugene have decided to leave Guadalupe and, although Antonio's parents try to persuade them to stay, they are both gone when Antonio wakes in the morning. Antonio's mother blames the wildness of the Marez blood, and Antonio's father realizes that he will never be able to fulfill his dream of moving to California. Andrew is the only one who has decided to stay, and he tells Antonio that he will study for his high school diploma and get a job in town.

Back at school, Antonio continues to excel in his studies and, by the end of the year, he has improved so much that he is promoted to the third grade. Thrilled at his success in school, Antonio decides to go fishing with Samuel before heading home. As they fish, Samuel tells Antonio the story of the golden carp. Many years ago, a people had lived in the land and enjoyed much prosperity. The only thing that the gods had forbidden for them to eat was the carp in the river. After forty years of drought, all of the plants in the land had died, and the people were forced to catch and eat the carp in the river to survive. The gods were so angry that they turned all of the people into carp and doomed them to live in the river for the rest of eternity. One of the gods took pity on his people and asked to be turned in a carp so that he could protect them. Antonio asks if the golden carp is still in the river, and Samuel tells him that, once the summer begins, his friend Cico will find Antonio and show him the golden carp to see for himself.

That summer, Antonio spends every day fishing by the river and waiting for Cico to find him and show him the golden carp. He hears rumors that his uncle Lucas has been cursed and, one morning, his uncle Pedro arrives to ask Ultima for help. According to Uncle Pedro, Lucas had interrupted the evil Trementina sisters while they were in the middle of the Black Mass. To punish him, they had cursed him with a terrible sickness, and he was now near death. Ultima warns Antonio's parents that they could set a chain of events into motion if they ask her to cure Lucas but then agrees to take the case if Antonio will be her assistant.

Ultima and Antonio travel to El Puerto de los Lunas and arrive at a proper fee for the cure with Antonio's grandfather. Ultima confronts Tenorio Trementina at his bar and warns him to tell his daughters to lift the curse on Lucas or face the consequences. On their way home, Antonio is nearly trampled by Tenorio on horseback, racing home to warn his daughters of Ultima's involvement. Once back at the Luna farm, Ultima closes herself into Lucas' room with Antonio and begins to treat Lucas, forcing a mixture of kerosene and herbs down his throat.

While Ultima is working on Lucas, the Trementina sisters attack the house in the form of coyotes but are chased away by Ultima's owl. Antonio falls into a trance and begins to assume characteristics of Lucas' illness; Ultima uses Antonio's healthy body as a surrogate for his uncle's weak body, making it easier to remove the curse. Ultima continues to give Lucas herbal remedies and then makes three clay dolls covered in wax to represent the Trementina sisters in a ritual to extricate the curse from Lucas. She sticks pins in the dolls, and Lucas vomits up green bile and a huge ball of squirming hair. When Lucas is able to eat a bowl of atole, Ultima pronounces him cured. On the way home, Ultima stops in the woods where the Trementina sisters performed their satanic rites and burns the evil ball of hair.

Analysis:

Antonio's time at school becomes increasingly important as a way for him to mark his independence from his family. Not only is Antonio learning the magic of letters at school, he is making new friends and developing relationships with people outside of his parents. Characters like Samuel help Antonio begin to develop his own identity and start to explore ideas that he had never before considered. One such idea, prompted by Samuel's story about the golden carp, is that Antonio's mother might be worshipping the wrong god. Although Antonio is still closely connected to his family, his time at school sets him on his way to become a man of learning. Instead of just learning letters and numbers, however, Antonio is learning about new cultures, new people, and new faiths. He is also developing the ability to make his own decisions. Even a decision as small as choosing to go fishing with Samuel instead of going straight home is significant in this framework.

Antonio's dream at the beginning of Chapter 9 emphasizes that he is still somewhat anxious about his future as a man of learning. In the dream, both Antonio's mother and his priest inform him that he will lose his innocence as soon as he gains understanding. Antonio loves to learn and is enthusiastic about his progress at school, but, at the same time, he fears that his success in academics will go hand-in-hand with a loss of innocence.

In this dream Antonio also recognizes a relationship between physical pleasure and a loss of innocence. Because he might be a priest, Antonio believes that he must abstain from all physical pleasures, particularly those that would take place in Rosie's brothel. His brothers argue that a priest is still a man with desires, but Antonio is unable to accept the idea. If he is to be a man of learning who learns from his experiences, Antonio fears that he will never be able to maintain his innocence and become a priest.

Andrew's agreement to wait until Antonio has lost his innocence is also significant. While Antonio feels abandoned and confused by his other two brothers, as well as by his mother and his priest, he still is able to look up to Andrew as a model of adulthood. In Antonio's eyes, Andrew is the only figure in his life that has been able to reconcile knowledge with innocence; he is the only brother who is not yet "lost."

Antonio's questions about sin and knowledge also translate into his questions about the golden carp and Catholicism. After Samuel's description of the myth, Antonio begins to doubt aspects of Christianity for the first time. He wonders if his mother is completely accurate in her faith and begins to become more independent in his thinking. Antonio's questions about Catholicism coincide with Ultima's successful treatment of Uncle Lucas. Antonio is very cognizant of the failure of the priest to cure Uncle Lucas and doubts the efficacy of Christianity in the face of Ultima's superior skill.

Antonio is further drawn into the world of superstition, healing, and pagan beliefs by his personal involvement in Ultima's treatment. Antonio acts as a sort of medium for Ultima's power and takes on his uncle's symptoms in an effort to ground him in the Luna blood. Antonio's spiritual nature is further suggested by his middle name, Juan, which is said to have many mystical associations in Mexican culture. Because Antonio has such a strong connection to this mystical culture, his nature is called into question. Just as Ultima is a combination of good and evil because of her blend of Catholic beliefs and ritualistic pagan actions, Antonio appears to be an amalgamation of both cultures. With this in mind, Antonio must reconcile both the conflicting cultures that surround his life and the conflicting cultures that make up his character.

Summary and Analysis of Chapter 11-13 (Once-Trece)

Antonio is fishing and wondering why Ultima was able to cure Lucas when the priest could not. He hears someone calling him and discovers Cico, the boy who Samuel had promised would take him to see the golden carp. Cico offers to show Antonio the golden carp, and Antonio enthusiastically agrees. His only concern is that he is Christian, and he does not know if he is allowed to believe that the golden carp is a god as Cico does. Cico makes Antonio swear an oath that he will never kill a carp and then leads him off into the direction of the carp.

On the way, Cico takes Antonio into a beautiful luscious garden that is owned and tended by Narciso. Antonio is amazed that Narciso has such a close connection to the earth and grows such beautiful plants even though the town people mock him for being a drunk. Cico and Antonio also run into some of Antonio's friends while they are playing basketball, and they taunt Antonio about his relationship to Ultima and ask him to do magic. Upset at their accusations about Ultima, Antonio agrees to do magic and throws up on the basketball court. Laughing at the looks on his friends' faces, Antonio leaves again with Cico. After walking further than Antonio had ever walked in the hills, the boys crawl through a thicket and come upon a large hidden pond where Antonio sees the glorious golden carp for the first time.

Cico tells Antonio about the golden carp's prophecy that the weight of people's sins will one day cause the land to sink deep into the earth. Antonio argues that the prophecy is unjust because everyone will be punished for the sins of a few people. Cico replies that every person sins. Antonio is deeply saddened by this knowledge and returns home to ask Ultima about the golden carp and what he should believe. Ultima asserts that she cannot tell him what he should believe. Instead, as Antonio grows up, he will have to find his own truths for himself.

That night, Antonio has another dream about the conflicting cultures in his life, first about the clash between Christianity and the beliefs of the golden carp and then about the tension between his Luna family and his Marez family. At the end of the dream, Ultima appears and assures Antonio that he contains elements of both sides of his family.

Later in the summer, Antonio's parents are still trying to cope with the unbalance in their family. Antonio's father drinks constantly and is extremely upset that his dream of California has been destroyed. Antonio's mother is equally depressed and tries to comfort herself with the fact that Andrew is still at home. Antonio continues to spend most of his time with Ultima and begins to feel even more attached to her than he is to his mother. One day, Antonio notices the three wax-covered clay dolls in Ultima's room. Ultima forbids him to touch the dolls and then gives him a strict warning to stay aware from Tenorio Trementina if Antonio should see him. She then gives Antonio her scapular, a pouch of dried herbs, for additional protection.

One night, Narciso bursts into the house, warning the family that one of Tenorio's daughters has died and that Tenorio is out for revenge. Narciso also explains that Tenorio has accused Ultima of performing witchcraft and raised a drunken mob to capture her. At that moment, the angry mob reaches the house, and Antonio's father demands that they explain their reasons for trespassing. The mob begins to feel ashamed in front of Gabriel, but Tenorio upholds his accusation and demands that they give him Ultima.

Narciso offers a compromise, suggesting that they make Ultima undergo a test for witchcraft: if she is unable to pass through a doorway marked with a cross made out of needles, she is proven to be a witch. The mob agrees to abide by the result of this test. Suddenly Ultima's owl swoops onto Tenorio and claws out one of his eyes. When everyone looks back at the doorway, Ultima has passed through and proven that she is not a witch. The mob breaks up but Tenorio still promises that he will kill Ultima. Before Antonio goes inside to bed, he notices that the holy cross on the door has fallen on the ground. He does not know if it fell or if someone knocked it down.

The next morning, Uncle Pedro arrives and the family goes for their annual vacation at El Puerto to help with the harvest. This time, Antonio's father agrees to accompany the family as well. Although no one speaks openly about the events of the night before, Gabriel secretly tells Antonio's mother that Tenorio has lost one of his eyes from the owl attack and that the priest has refused to give his dead daughter a proper Christian mass. As they drive to the farm, Antonio has time to think about the golden carp and its differences from the doctrine of the Catholic Church. Antonio wishes that it were possible to find a god who was always forgiving.

Antonio asks his uncle why the Lunas did not warn Ultima of Tenorio's rampage. Pedro is disconcerted by the question and eventually explains that Antonio's grandfather did not want them to become involved, despite the fact that Ultima had saved Lucas' life. Antonio criticizes his uncle for this decision, and Pedro admits that he is ashamed of his cowardice. He promises that he will stand by Ultima in the future.

After they are settled at El Puerto, Uncle Mateo and the other adults discuss the latest news of Tenorio and his daughters. Because the priest has refused to allow Tenorio's daughter to be buried in holy ground, her sisters will weave a coffin of cottonwood branches for her body and perform a black mass. When Antonio falls asleep, he dreams of the witches' black mass and sees the cottonwood coffin. But when he looks inside the coffin, Antonio is horrified to see Ultima's body.

The next morning, Antonio and the rest of the family watch the funeral procession for Tenorio's daughter. Tenorio leads the procession to the church in an effort to force the priest to allow his daughter the holy Christian rites, but the priest refuses and excommunicates Tenorio and his two daughters in front of the entire town. Although Tenorio will no longer be able to rally the rest of the town to pursue Ultima, his thirst for revenge against her has only increased with this blow.

Analysis:

Antonio's interaction with his friends at the basketball court demonstrates the view toward Ultima shared by the people in the town. The majority of the townspeople believe that Ultima practices witchcraft and, whether it this craft has good intentions or not, she is still a bruja. Ultima, then, is prey to the fear of difference as well as the ubiquitousness of rumors. Antonio has never been fully exposed to this feeling of guilt by association, and he is sickened by the accusations of his friends.

Similarly, Antonio's discovery of Narciso's garden forces him to reconsider the common perceptions of Narciso as a worthless drunk. Antonio had never come into close contact with Narciso and had always accepted the town's perspective as accurate. When he sees Narciso's beautiful garden with Cico, Antonio realizes that there is more to Narciso than meets the eye. Although he is technically a vaquero like Antonio's father, Narciso also exhibits the characteristics of Luna in the connection that he shares with the earth and with nature. In Narciso, Antonio finally has an example of a person who blends both cultures in his life. Unfortunately, even as Narciso is able to successfully balance these conflicting cultures, he is still isolated from the rest of the town and only has Cico and a few others for support.

When Antonio sees the golden carp for the first time, he finally feels a true connection to nature. This harmony with nature is broken as soon as Antonio introduces the thought of Christianity into the scene: at the precise moment that Antonio begins to think about God and sin, the black bass breaks through the water as a clear symbol of evil and sin. Antonio hopes that his first communion will be as harmonious as his first experience with the golden carp, but the appearance of the black bass suggests that this will not be the case.

When Antonio notices his parents' unhappiness, he discovers the inevitable nature of change in life. His brothers' decision to leave Guadalupe has resulted in his parents' unhappiness, but Antonio begins to realize that they needed to find their own independent lives. He understands that he may eventually cause the same grief and sadness in his parents when he becomes an adult, but this transition is a natural part of life.

The sadness of Antonio's father, in particular, demonstrates a personal epiphany about his sons' character and the Marez family. He always hoped that his sons would exhibit the characteristics of a Marez but never realized that their Marez blood would lead them away from home. He cannot fault Leon and Eugene for their departure; the wildness in their Marez blood already determined their paths, long before they returned from the war. Gabriel now realizes that he must admire them for their rebellion because it is a quality that he shares, and he can only hope that they will be happy in their independent lives.

When Tenorio and the mob come to the Marez house, we see a glimpse of the superstitious fear of witchcraft that permeates the culture of the town. The men in the mob allow themselves to be stirred into a frenzy because they are afraid of what they do not understand. The test for witchcraft is an opportunity to place Ultima in a definable position: either she is a witch, or she is not a witch. Although the mob is eventually satisfied that she is not a witch, Antonio notices that Ultima cannot be defined by such a test. The fact that Antonio finds the cross of needles on the ground demonstrates that Ultima has not necessarily even taken the test for witchcraft. Above all, she cannot be characterized as one thing or the other because she is a blend of many cultures and many beliefs.

Summary and Analysis of Chapters 14-16 (Catorce-Dieciséis)

After the harvest has ended, Antonio returns to school and tells Samuel that he has seen the golden carp. Samuel is very pleased but warns Antonio that his classmates will not understand his family's defense of an accused witch. At the schoolyard, Ernie and some of the other boys accuse Antonio of living with a witch and Antonio gets into a fight with them. After the teachers break up the fight, the boys go into their classes, and no one taunts Antonio about Ultima again.

There is a terrible blizzard on the scheduled day of the Christmas pageant at school. Although Antonio's sisters stay home, Antonio decides to brave the blizzard in order to participate in the school play. Antonio and the rest of his friends are the only students to arrive at school, but Miss Violet decides to perform the Christmas pageant anyway, resulting in a chaotic and disastrous scene.

On his way home after the play, Antonio sees Tenorio and Narciso fighting in the street. Eventually Tenorio runs off, vowing to kill both Narciso and Ultima. Determined to warn Ultima of this danger, the badly injured Narciso staggers to Rosie's brothel and calls Andrew to the door to help him. Andrew, preoccupied with one of Rosie's girls, scoffs at Narciso's concern and goes back inside. Narciso decides to warn Ultima on his own and sets off for the Marez house, still unaware that Antonio is following him. On his way to the Marez house, Tenorio ambushes Narciso and shoots him. After Tenorio flees, Antonio kneels beside Narciso as he lays dying and agrees to hear his last confession.

Antonio runs to his house and tells his family what has happened. Overcome with fever, Antonio dreams of his brother being pulled into the fires of hell by the girl at Rosie's. In his dream, Antonio begs God to forgive Andrew of his sins, and a voice replies that Andrew can be forgiven only if Tenorio is forgiven as well. Antonio sees the blood of Narciso and the blood of Lupito mix in the river and watches in horror as a giant mob demands Ultima's blood. Antonio's three brothers appear and then transform into the Trementina sisters and place a curse on Antonio. As Antonio dies from the curse, he sees the mob kill Ultima and his family and eat the forbidden carp from the river. He hears a thundering of the earth and watches as a huge rift opens and swallows the town of Guadalupe. The Luna farmers from El Puerto arrive and bury the ashes of Antonio's family. The golden carp appears and swallows all of the ash and sinners still left in the world and brings forth a new pure world under a new sun.

After his fever breaks, Antonio remains bedridden for several days, still weak from pneumonia. He discovers that his father had found Narciso's body and accused Tenorio of murder. Unfortunately, because the only witness was a seven year old boy, the coroner ultimately decides that Narciso's death was accidental. When Andrew comes to visit Antonio in his sickroom, he seems ill-at-ease, and Antonio wonders if he betrayed his brother's secret about Rosie's. Ultima assures Antonio that he did not expose Andrew during his fever.

After Antonio recovers, he spends most of his Christmas vacation listening to Ultima's stories and reciting his catechism in Spanish and English with his mother. Eugene and Leon visit the family during Christmas vacation after being brought home in a police car; while they were driving from Las Vegas, they totaled their car and were forced to burn it to stay warm. Eugene, Leon and Andrew spend the evening playing pool in town, and Antonio's father feels increasing bitterness about the wandering Marez blood in his sons. Even though Eugene and Leon are back, Gabriel knows that they will soon leave again. The following day, Leon and Eugene leave for Santa Fe, this time taking Andrew with them.

Spring arrives, and Antonio goes back to school. He feels older, weighted down by his experience with Narciso's death and does not understand why Tenorio remains unpunished for his crimes. Antonio hopes that all of his questions will finally be answered by his first Communion.

On the way home from school, Antonio is confronted by an enraged Tenorio. The second of Tenorio's three daughters is now dying, and Tenorio swears that he will kill Ultima. Tenorio leaves without hurting him, and Antonio quickly runs home to tell Ultima what has happened. Ultima reassures Antonio that she is prepared for her enemy and that Tenorio will not be able to ambush her as easily as he did Narciso.

Analysis:

Antonio's fight with his classmates demonstrates another example of the mob mentality that Antonio is beginning to understand. Just as Tenorio's mob was eager to accuse Ultima of being a witch, Antonio's classmates quickly band together to taunt Antonio about Ultima. With each additional conflict of ideas that Antonio faces, he becomes more and more aware of the numerous perspectives that shape the truth in the world. Although Antonio's friends still believe that Ultima is a witch, his willingness to fight his friends in her defense convinces them to leave him alone. Anaya introduces the farce of the Christmas pageant to provide some comic relief. This scene is one of the few comic moments in the novel, and it provides the readers with some insight into the less traumatic life experiences that also make up Antonio's development.

When Antonio sees Andrew at Rosie's brothel, he feels betrayed on many levels. First of all, Antonio realizes that his idealized vision of his brother is illusory: Andrew is just as "lost" as his other brothers. Moreover, Antonio feels the loss of his own innocence. In one of his earlier dreams, Andrew had promised to wait to enter Rosie's until Antonio loses his innocence. Because Andrew has been sinning at Rosie's, Antonio must conclude that his innocence has been lost.

Andrew's inaction despite Narciso's request also provides some insight into his later behavior. Because of Andrew's laziness, Narciso is murdered by Tenorio and Antonio is forced to witness yet another traumatic moment. Andrew feels terrible guilt at what he is done and feels the loss of his former close relationship with Antonio. This palpable loss of Antonio's respect and approval proves to Andrew that his efforts to stay in Guadalupe are hopeless. By moving to Santa Fe with his other brothers, Andrew demonstrates that his loss of innocence is truly complete.

Narciso's murder forces Antonio to come to grips with more questions about sin and punishment. He is forced to assume the position of a priest to take Narciso's last confession even though he feels unworthy and extremely uncomfortable. Antonio is also unable to figure out why God does not punish Tenorio for his crime against Narciso. This concern, then, prompts Antonio's eighth dream in which Antonio attempts to garner salvation for his family. The voice of Heaven points out that Antonio asks for forgiveness for some and for punishment for others, something that is impossible. In the next part of the dream, Antonio witnesses the apocalypse prophesied by the golden carp; he and his family members are murdered by an evil mob, and everyone from the town is destroyed. Yet, Antonio's vision ends with hope as the golden carp establishes a new world to make up for the old. In this view, the golden carp allows for both punishment and forgiveness and destroys the entire world only so that it can be remade in purity.

The town's dismissal of Narciso's death also introduces Antonio to the injustices that are prompted by prejudice. Because the entire town views Narciso as a drunk, they do not deem him worthy of an investigation for a so-called "murder." Although all of the evidence is against it, the coroner categorizes the murder as an accident and ensures that Narciso will not receive any legal justice. Antonio also learns that Narciso's drunkenness is the result of hardship and unhappiness in his life, a fact that the townspeople did not consider when branding Narciso as a drunk.

Summary and Analysis of Chapters 17-19 (Diecisiete-Diecinueve)

In March, dust storms begin to plague the area. Antonio overhears adults blaming the unusual storms to the atomic testing taking place nearby. Antonio's father laughs at these claims and informs Antonio that the dust storms are the voice of the llano, informing the people that they have used up too many of their resources in overgrazing.

Antonio and his classmates begin to take catechism lessons in preparation for their first Communion. Antonio continues to wonder about the nature of sin and punishment in the world and anxiously awaits the moment when he will receive the knowledge of God. He is convinced that he will finally hear God's voice and the answers to all of his questions when he takes Communion for the first time.

At the same time, Antonio is perplexed by Florence's persistent atheism. Although Florence attends catechism to be with his friends, he does not believe a compassionate God cannot exist in a world that has so much sadness and evil. Explaining that both of his parents are dead and his sisters work as prostitutes in Rosie's, Florence asks Antonio how God could place so many hardships in his life. Antonio is unable to answer because Florence is articulating many of the same questions that Antonio ponders himself. While they are having this discussion, Antonio and Florence realize that they are late for catechism and hurry inside the church. Once they are inside, Father Byrnes punishes Florence for tardiness but excuses Antonio.

During the catechism lesson, Father Byrnes uses a frightening analogy to explain the length of eternity. He tells them to imagine that they must move a massive pile of sand across an ocean with only a tiny bird. The bird can only take one grain of sand in its beak at a time. When the bird successfully moves the entire pile of sand across the ocean, Father Byrnes explains, it has only been the first day of eternity. As he listens to Father Byrnes' explanation, Antonio realizes that Florence is not afraid of the punishment awaiting atheists and will be doomed to an eternity in Hell. Antonio sees visions of Florence burning in eternal flames and yet still refusing to accept the existence of God. Antonio and Samuel decide that they will introduce Florence to the golden carp the next summer. If anything, Florence will at least be able to have faith in a god, even if it is not a Christian god.

On the day before Easter, Antonio is preparing to make his first confession. His mother has bought him a new suit for the occasion, and Antonio quickly runs down to the church with Samuel to wait for his turn. While he is waiting, the other boys demand that Antonio pretends to be a priest so they can make their confessions to him. Horse confesses that he made a hole in the wall of the girl's bathroom so that he could watch them and Bones confesses that he saw a high school couple having sex. Antonio gives both boys an equal penance. The children then force Florence to "play" the game and confess his sins. Florence refuses, declaring that he has not sinned against God, but God has sinned against him. Horrified at this blasphemy, the children demand that Antonio "sentence" Florence to death. Antonio refuses and instead forgives Florence for his sins. Angry at Antonio's show of favoritism to an atheist, the children tear off his new jacket and beat him. When the priest calls Antonio for confession, the other children let him go, and Florence asks Antonio why he did not give him a penance. He then concludes by asserting that Antonio could never be a priest to his classmates.

On Easter Sunday, Antonio is breathless with excitement at the prospect of finally understanding God. When the priest places the Communion wafer in Antonio's mouth, Antonio expects to hear God's voice speak to him and answer his questions. Instead, Antonio hears nothing but silence.

Analysis:

Antonio is exposed to injustice in the framework of the church itself when he observes Father Byrnes' unjust punishment of Florence for tardiness. Father Byrnes is biased against Florence while he favors Antonio, and Antonio begins to question his faith in organized religion. He realizes that a person like Father Byrnes may live according to the laws of Christianity and preach catechism, but he is not necessarily a good Christian or a good moral compass.

Antonio's discussions with Florence force him to realize the rational problems with Christianity. Although he wants to convince Florence that his beliefs are correct, Antonio cannot deny Florence's logic. Because Florence's arguments make him more confused, Antonio places even more hope on his first Communion as being the key to his understanding of God. The clear-cut questions and answers that he learns in catechism makes Antonio expect his conversation with God to be equally simple. As a child, he has unquestioning faith that his Communion will lead to a sort of religious realization and all of his questions will be answered.

When Antonio takes Communion, however, he discovers that he is no closer to understanding God than he was before. He realizes that his faith in God was unfounded, and he now must rely on his own moral judgment to answer his questions about sin and punishment. Antonio even begins to question that God exists, a possibility that becomes increasingly likely to him as the book goes on.

During Antonio's process of catechism and Communion, he is also forced to take on the role of a priest another time. With Narciso's last confession, Antonio simply listened as a figure of comfort, but in this scene, Antonio must actually pass judgment on his peers and the sins that they have committed. Because Antonio does not force Florence to do penance for his blasphemy, Antonio is essentially cast out by his group. In yet another example of mob mentality and prejudice, the other boys are not able to accept someone with differing religious beliefs. When Antonio does not go along with their plan to punish Florence, Antonio is choosing the wrong side.

Similar to the way that Antonio once viewed good and evil as totally distinct entities, Antonio's friends are unable to accept the possibility that an atheist can have logical arguments.

Florence's declaration that Antonio will never be their priest is actually a compliment that demonstrates Antonio's increasing independence. Antonio has the capacity to make his own moral decisions and he will never be forced to take on the beliefs of a community, just as he refused to follow his friends' plan to punish Florence. This strength of character highlights Antonio's growth as an individual, as well as his ability to function morally as an isolated figure. Florence does not mean to say that Antonio would be a bad priest, but rather that his classmates are not yet able to accept the type of priest that he will ultimately become.

Summary and Analysis of Chapters 20-22 (Veinte-Veintidós)

After Easter, Antonio continues to take communion in church, but he is not satisfied. On the last day of school, Antonio challenges the Vitamin Kid to race across the bridge as they always do. But this time, the Vitamin Kid does not try to race with Antonio and instead walks calmly alongside a girl named Ida. Although Antonio knows that he has finally beaten the fastest runner in the town, he does not feel happy in his victory.

As the summer days pass, Antonio notices that Ultima's owl is making cries of warning every night instead of the gentle hooting of the previous summer. Ultima tells Antonio not to worry about it, but Antonio is not comforted. Antonio overhears rumors that Tenorio's second daughter is now dying, and he worries that Tenorio will finally fulfill his vow to kill Ultima. One day, Téllez, a friend of Antonio's father, comes to ask Ultima for help in removing a curse that has been laid on his house. Téllez believes that the house is possessed: pots and pans fly across the room and stones fall from the sky onto the roof. The local priest was unable to lift the curse, and Téllez views Ultima as his last hope. Ultima agrees to help and explains that the Trementina sisters have awoken the ghosts of three ancient Comanches and forced them to do evil to the Téllez family.

Antonio and his father accompany Ultima to the house to help lift the curse. When they arrive, Ultima orders Antonio and Gabriel to build a platform of cedar posts and place juniper branches on the top. While they are building it, Ultima herds the family back into the house, and Antonio hears her chanting for several hours. When Ultima emerges from the house, she is carrying three mysterious bundles to burn on the cedar platform. She declares that the curse has been lifted but that Téllez should avoid Tenorio at any cost. When Ultima mentions his name, Téllez remembers that he had had a confrontation with Tenorio a few weeks earlier and realizes that he and his daughters have been the source of the curse.

That night, Antonio dreams of his three brothers wandering in a foreign city. They beg him to release them from their wild Marez blood, but Antonio tells them that he cannot help them. He removes their livers from their bodies and places them on a fishing hook. His brothers suffer so earnestly that Antonio removes their lives from the hook and throws them into the River of the Carp. Only then are his brothers able to rest.

Later in the summer, Cico and Antonio walk toward the secret creek so that they can see the golden carp. As they wait, Antonio thinks about God's failure to communicate with him during Communion. He wonders if God is still alive or if God ever was alive, remembering all of the times when God has failed where Ultima has succeeded. The golden carp arrives, and Antonio is transfixed with its beauty. Then he remembers that he wanted to tell Florence about the golden carp, and he and

Cico leave to find Florence. As they walk near the concrete spillway, they see Horse and Antonio's other classmates waving frantically at them: Florence had dove into the water in the spillway ten minutes before and still had not come up. Cico is about to dive into the water to find him when they see Florence's body slowly rise to the surface; he is dead. As a crowd forms around the body, Antonio tries to prayer an Act of Contrition for Florence, but he knows that it is useless because Florence was an atheist. Antonio notices that Cico has disappeared and, as Horse and Bones enthusiastically answer questions from the crowd, he runs to the river to escape the sick feeling in his stomach.

That night, Antonio dreams of Narciso, Lupito, and Florence, the three people that he seen die and prayed the Act of Contrition for. He asks why he must be witness to so much violence, and a voice replies that creation lies in violence. He watches as a priest desecrates the altar with pigeon blood, Cico kills the golden carp with his spear, and Tenorio kills Ultima. Antonio is desolate and asks God why He has forsaken him. Antonio awakes from his nightmare to find himself in Ultima's arms. Ultima gives him a potion to make him sleep without any dreams.

The next day, Antonio does not go to Florence's funeral; he does not feel that he can be comforted by church when God leaves Florence to wander without peace because he did not accept Communion. Ultima suggests that Antonio should spend the rest of the summer with the Lunas at El Puerto, and his parents agree, hoping that Antonio will be able to cope with his grief when he is not surrounded by the memories of his friend. Antonio's father drives him to El Puerto and explains that it will be good for Antonio to be in the company of men who can guide him in his development. Gabriel acknowledges that the ways of the vaquero are ending and thinks that it might be time to end the conflict between the Marez and the Lunas. Antonio must take the good characteristics of the Marez and combine them with the good characteristics of the Lunas, just as he must combine different religious beliefs to create his own personal faith. Gabriel also explains that most of the things that are seen as "evil" are not actually evil; they are just things that people do not understand. Understanding, he asserts, does not necessarily come with taking Communion, but rather with life experiences. Because Ultima understands so much from her experiences in life, she is able to touch the souls of sick people and heal them.

During his time at El Puerto, Antonio no longer suffers from nightmares, and he learns a great deal about farming and Luna beliefs from his uncles. His future may be uncertain, but Antonio is happy to be familiar with the lifestyle of the Lunas and recognizes that he could be happy as a farmer if he chose that path. Near the end of the summer, Antonio learns that his parents will be arriving within a few days to take him home. His uncle Pedro informs him that he and his brothers have been very pleased with his progress over the summer and are happy to have a man of education among the Lunas. Antonio asserts that he is also a Marez, and Pedro agrees, restating their pride in his accomplishment. Their conversation is interrupted by Uncle Juan who informs Pedro that Tenorio's second daughter has died, and Tenorio has vowed to kill Ultima. Juan is hesitant to become involved, but Pedro reminds him of their debt to Ultima for saving Lucas' life and is determined to warn her. Pedro tells Antonio to go back to the farm and back up his belongings; he will take Antonio back to Guadalupe that night.

As Antonio walks across the bridge to his grandfather's house, he is almost trampled by Tenorio and his horse. Tenorio is drunk and determined to kill Antonio if he can. Antonio escapes by jumping into the embankment, and Tenorio taunts him by telling him that he will kill Ultima's owl and thus kill Ultima herself. Antonio finally understands that the owl is Ultima's spirit and soul, and he is suddenly frightened for Ultima's life. Unable to cross the bridge with Tenorio trapping him, Antonio decides to run straight to Guadalupe to warn Ultima. After many miles, Antonio finally reaches home just in time to see Tenorio shoot Ultima's owl with his rifle. Triumphant at his success in killing the owl, Tenorio turns to shoot Antonio in the forehead, but Uncle Pedro kills Tenorio before he can pull the trigger.

Antonio finds the dying owl on the ground and, wrapping it in a blanket, rushes to Ultima's room. Finding her dying in her bed, Antonio kneels beside her and begs her not to die. Ultima explains that her teacher taught her to perform good works without interfering with destiny and upsetting the balance of the world. When she and Tenorio are both dead, the balance will be restored. She accepts her death because it means that she helped others to live. Ultima asks Antonio to burn all of her possessions and to bury the owl underneath a forked juniper tree. Antonio agrees, but asks Ultima to bless him before he goes. Ultima blesses him "in the name of all that is good and strong and beautiful." Antonio buries the owl under a forked juniper tree and returns after Ultima's body has been taken away. The next day, the town holds a funeral for Ultima and buries her body in the cemetery, but Antonio knows that he has already buried Ultima's true spirit beneath the juniper tree.

Analysis:

Antonio is growing up, and he begins to realize that growth and development are often accompanied by sadness and regret. When he tries to race the Vitamin Kid over the bridge but the Vitamin Kid is no longer interested, Antonio recognizes that something has been lost; he and friends are leaving their childhoods behind. Antonio must come to grips with the fact that change is always a factor in life, even when it brings sadness with it. Antonio's dream about his three brothers highlights this realization as Antonio accepts that his brothers must be wanderers. The fact that Antonio is the source of some of their pain also demonstrates his gradual acceptance that he has lost his innocence and is capable of committing sins against others.

Antonio was forced to mature quickly when he observed the deaths of Lupito and Narciso, but Florence's death is even more difficult to take. Because he knows that Florence did not believe in God, Antonio cannot find solace from his grief in the same ways that he dealt with Lupito and Narciso. He knows that Catholic doctrine dictates that Florence will either burn in Hell or simply wander the world, never to be at peace. Antonio knows that Florence was a good person, and he only wishes that he could have shown Florence the golden carp before his death.

Antonio continues to be preoccupied with questions about God, but he has given up waiting for God to speak to him through Communion. He continues to go to confession and take Communion, but he has also decided that he must find the answers to these questions from other sources. Although he still acknowledges that God determines who will go to Heaven and Hell, Antonio no longer believes that God is involved in the occurrences of daily life. This realization draws Antonio to the golden carp for a different kind of understanding of the world. While he is waiting to see the golden carp with Cico, Antonio finally feels an inner peace that he cannot find through Catholicism. Antonio has finally discovered a way to reconcile his conflicting religions as different perspectives of the same world. When one belief cannot answer all of his questions, Antonio knows to seek other sources until he has all of the understanding that he desires.

Antonio's drive to El Puerto with his father reveals that Gabriel Marez has also realized that a person should not think only in terms of one perspective. All beliefs and ideas are a matter of perspective, just as the concepts of good and evil are dependent on the beliefs of individual people. Every person builds their character according to their experiences in life, and this type of development ensures that a person cannot think in terms of absolutes.

In Antonio's final dream in the novel, he sees the three individuals that he was unable to save from death and prayed for in his innocence. The figures show each of Antonio's three faiths in life as they are desecrated and destroyed: the Catholic priest defiles the altar, the golden carp is killed, and Ultima is murdered. This destruction of Antonio's faith represents the darkest point in his religious beliefs when he no longer has anything to believe in. Yet, the voice from Heaven insists that violence and change are linked to creation. This declaration echoes the theme of growth and personal development that is emphasized throughout the novel. When Ultima dies, Antonio is finally able to understand this link between change and violence. His time working on the Luna farm has taught him the importance of harmony in nature, and he realizes that Ultima's death will reinstate the natural harmony of the world. He no longer fears death because he knows that it is a natural cycle of life and a change that is necessary for life to continue.

Suggested Essay Questions

1. What tensions are created for Antonio in his life because of his parents' different backgrounds?

Because Antonio's mother is a Luna and his father is a Marez, Antonio is born into a ready conflict between the two families. While his mother hopes that he will become a priest, a hope that is shared by Antonio's Luna uncles, his father hopes that he will become a vaquero like the Marez. This tension between the families is highlighted by the conflict that arises at the moment of Antonio's birth and causes him a great deal of anxiety about his purpose in life. Although Antonio does not want to disappoint either of his parents, he must eventually choose his own path.

2. Is the novel a romance, a fantasy, or a realistic life story? Why?

The novel contains elements of all of these types of stories. It is a very realistic life story because it follows the growth of its young protagonist as he deals with real life issues. It is also based on the author's actual childhood. At the same time, the novel contains many elements of fantasy and magic, with the myth of the Golden Carp, the good magic of Ultima, and the black magic of the Trementina sisters. Finally, the novel is also a romance novel because it is centered on the relationship between Antonio and Ultima and traces their development and growth. Therefore, although the novel is, at its center, a realistic coming-of-age story, it still contains all of the romance and magic of the myths that it describes.

3. What are the events in the book that change Antonio's life the most? What are they and why are they so important?

The deaths of Lupito, Narciso, and Florence are significant life-changing events for Antonio. The death of Lupito is particularly significant because it is the first death Antonio has witnessed, and it inspires his first questions about sin, death, and morality. Although these experiences are the most obvious choices, the novel also contains other experiences which could be read as being equally life-changing. Antonio's first experience with the Golden Carp is very important because it helps him to develop a new faith and begin to question the restrictions of Catholicism. Similarly, Antonio's presence when Ultima lifts the curse from Uncle Lucas provides Antonio with his first clear insight to the world of magic and pagan healing. Finally, Ultima's death and Antonio's burial of the owl can also be read as a crucial life-changing experience because of Antonio's eventual understanding that he must follow his own path in life.

4. What is the importance of dreams in the novel? Which dream is the most important to Antonio is his questions about life?

Antonio has several dreams throughout the novel, each of which highlight his particular anxiety or obsession at the time. His dreams provide key insights into his character because they allow the reader to mark the development of his character; his early dreams are concerned with his future and the conflict between the Luna and the Marez while his later dreams are apocalyptic and concerned with larger issues of morality. The most apocalyptic dream is also perhaps the most important dream in terms of Antonio's questions about life. In this dream, everything in the world is destroyed in horrific bloodshed, and the Golden Carp decides to give new birth and new purity to the world. Although Antonio is still fearful of sin and religion, this dream gives him new hope for a world of sinners.

5. What will Antonio become when he grows up? A priest? A vaquero? Why or why not?

Antonio's future is not clear because, at the end of the novel, he has finally decided to choose his own path. Instead of adhering to the beliefs of his mother or the desires of his father, he will fulfill Ultima's encouragement to follow his heart. With this in mind, it seems likely that Antonio will probably become a writer. At his birth, he reached out to the pen and paper, an action which, according to Ultima, will result in him becoming a man of learning. Whether or not this means that Antonio will become a priest as well is uncertain. Considering his questions about religion and morality and his anxieties about sin, it seems as if the life of a priest is not for him. However, no matter what he decides to do when he becomes an adult, the most important thing is that he has learned to make his own path.

6. What is the significance of Antonio discovering Andrew's presence at the brothel?

Andrew's presence at the brothel undercuts Antonio's view of his brother in several ways. First of all, Antonio makes a clear connection between sin and the brothel. Andrew's presence in the den of sin ruins Antonio's idealized view of him, particularly since he had always denied the idea that Andrew would keep company with prostitutes. Secondly, Andrew refusal to leave the brothel indirectly leads to Narciso's murder at Tenorio's hands. If Andrew had not been blinded by his lust and had accompanied Narciso, Narciso's death could have been avoided. Antonio cannot help but blame his brother for the second death of the book. Finally, Andrew's presence at the brothel undercuts one of Antonio's dream in which Andrew promised not to enter the brothel until Antonio had lost his innocence. Since Andrew has entered the brothel, Antonio must assume that he has also lost his own innocence.

7. How does the novel demonstrate the conflict between the doctrine of the Catholic Church and the pagan beliefs of the Golden Carp?

This tension is highlighted by the roles played by several characters in the book. Ultima, a figure that clearly corresponds to pagan beliefs and New Mexican myth, is set in opposition to Father Byrnes, the strict priest who upholds Catholic doctrine. Over the course of the book, both characters strive to teach Antonio their individual crafts, with Ultima introducing him to herbs, plants, and the presence of the river, and Father Byrnes teaching Antonio his catechism. Antonio's mother, a devoutly Catholic woman, is determined to make Antonio into a priest and is set in conflict with Antonio's father, who worships the earth and the sky as a true vaquero. The character of Florence is also extremely significant in emphasizing this conflict between religion and paganism. His insistence that a compassionate God cannot exist in the world sets Antonio at odds with his own Catholic upbringing and desire to help his friend find faith.

8. What is the significance of Antonio's age in the novel? How would the novel be different if he were older?

The novel is presented as a coming-of-age story in which the protagonist grows and develops as he experiences the tragedies of life. Another important theme of the novel is the question of sin and morality and the loss of innocence. At the beginning of the novel, Antonio is only six years old and very much a child in terms of understanding and innocence. Over the course of the novel, however, Antonio is exposed to events that force him to lose his innocence: the death of Lupito by the river, Narciso's murder by Tenorio, Florence's accidental drowning, and Ultima's death. Antonio must learn to reconcile this loss of innocence in order to become a man and follow his own path in life. Eventually, he is able to overcome his anxieties and realizes that a life of faith and a life of action are not mutually exclusive. Because this loss of innocence is a crucial element of the novel and Antonio's development as a character, the novel would not be as successful if he were older. Antonio's older brothers are already beyond this age of self-awareness, and it is important that Antonio is both self-aware and susceptible to change as an individual.

9. What is the role of women in the novel? Is the strongest character male or female?

The culture of Latino communities is patriarchal in nature, with men existing in the positions of power. Corresponding to that expectation, women do not place a hugely active role in the novel. Antonio's mother urges him to become a priest, but she does not have any power in the community or even the power to decide her son's future. Antonio's sisters are even more passive in the book; unlike Antonio's brothers who are very strong characters, his sisters are involved in very little of the plot. All of the important events in the novel (the death of Lupito; the murder of Narciso; Florence's drowning; the discovery of the Golden Carp) take place with limited or no female presence. The only exception to this rule is Ultima. Over all, Ultima is the strongest character in the book, and she ultimately teaches Antonio the most about life and the path to follow in his future. She also has the most power in the book and is able to use magic to lift curses and reinforce balance. Ultima's strength as a character is perhaps due to her position as a curandera. Although she is important in the community, her skills and power her from the rest of the town and ensure that she can never truly fit in with everyone else. In order for her to have power and exist as a strong female character, it seems that Ultima must lead an isolated existence.

10. What scene in the novel forces the readers to question Ultima's true nature? Why is this scene important?

Readers are forced to question Ultima's true nature in the scene when Tenorio and his mob accuse Ultima of witchcraft. They agree to test Ultima by placing a cross of needles above the doorway and seeing if she is able to pass through; if she cannot, they reason, she must be a witch. Ultima successfully passes through the doorway, but Antonio notices that the cross has fallen on the ground. It is unclear whether or not Ultima was truly able to pass through the doorway when it is marked with the holy cross. This realization forces Antonio to question the dichotomy between good and evil. Ultima performs good deeds, but she is still accused of being a witch. At the same time, Tenorio takes evil actions but cannot be blamed for seeking to avenge the deaths of his daughters. Antonio must ultimately conclude that a good person is one who acts according to the spirit of Catholicism, not necessary the person who upholds the law of Catholicism.

Aztec Mythology in Bless Me, Ultima

Myth plays a very prominent role in Bless Me, Ultima, both providing cultural background of the community described and directly helping Antonio in his individual development. The myth of the golden carp is certainly the most significant myth used in the novel, particularly because it helps to elucidate Antonio's increasing anxiety and eventual acceptance of the differing religious beliefs that he encounters. The book also contains more minor myths that serve the function of simply giving the reader a glimpse of Mexican-American culture. One example of this is Ultima's training in magic and beliefs in the harmony of the world. These myths and many other elements of the novel can be traced directly to the Aztec mythology that informs Mexican-American culture. An analysis of the myths Anaya uses becomes even more interesting when considering their origins in Aztec legend.

The myth of the golden carp finds its origins in a creation myth from Aztec culture, which was carried down to the Mexican communities of the present day. According to Aztec legend, there were four ages of the world or "suns" before the present world, each of which was destroyed by an individual apocalypse. The four ages were called "Tiger Sun," "Wind Sun," "Rain Sun," and "Water Sun." Although the progressive order of these worlds varies in different primary sources, the description of the "Water Sun" or "Atonatiuh" remains generally the same. According to this legend, the world was flooded with mighty waters, and all of the people were transformed into fish. A man and his wife survived the flood in a boat and became the parents of a new generation of people that would populate the fifth age of the world. The presence of this couple in the legend clearly relates to the Biblical story of Noah's Arc, but the similarities with Samuel's story of the golden carp are also undeniable.

Other elements in Anaya's novel also relate closely to Aztec mythology about the present age of the world. The fifth age of the world is known as "Nahui-Ollin," meaning "balance," and is ruled over by the gods Quetzalcoatl and Tezcatlipoca. The significance of balance in the world of the novel cannot be understated. Throughout Antonio's life, he attempts to create a balance between his religious beliefs, his family expectations, and the hopes of his mother and father. By the end of the novel, Antonio is able to reconcile all of the differences that he encounters and create a harmonious set of beliefs to guide his path in life. Moreover, Ultima herself asserts the importance of balance in their world as she lay dying. Because she and Tenorio upset the harmony of the world through their actions, both of their deaths were necessary in order to regain the natural balance. Ultima lived her life with the knowledge that balance must be maintained. Whenever she was unable to maintain the balance, she still chose to help others with the knowledge that her life would be sacrificed. Not only does Anaya highlight this belief in balance in Ultima's character, he emphasizes it as a constant theme throughout the book.

Anaya also incorporates the prophesied apocalypse of this fifth world into his novel.

In one of Antonio's nightmares, he watches as a huge chasm in the ground swallows up his town and destroys all of the sinners. According to Aztec beliefs, the fifth age of the world would eventually face destruction from a massive earthquake, just as Antonio foresees in his dream. At the end of his dream, Antonio sees the golden carp giving birth to a new world and a new sun. This cycle of destruction, rebirth, and regeneration mirrors the process of creation that is described by the Aztec myth. For each of the ages, destruction was soon followed by the creation of a new world and a new sun, a chance for the world to regenerate and try again.

The figures of Quetzalcoatl and Tezcatlipoca also appear indirectly in the themes of the book that relate to this fifth age. Quetzalcoatl, characterized as a combination of a bird and a serpent, was believed to be the god of the priests, as well as the god of learning and knowledge. He was also associated with farming, as the giver of maize, and with the cycle of life and death. Tezcatlipoca, on the other hand, was seen as the opposite of Quetzalcoatl in many ways. One of four Tezcatlipocas, the black Tezcatlipoca was associated with the night winds, hurricanes, the earth, strife, and night. Quetzalcoatl and Tezcatlipoca were constantly at odds. In fact, the destruction of each age was thought to be a result of their fighting: Tezcatlipoca ruled over the first age until Quetzacoatl destroyed it, Quetzacoatl ruled over the second age until Tezcatlipoca destroyed it, and so on.

The rivalry between these two gods, who jointly rule over the fifth age, has many similarities to the conflict between the Marez and the Lunas described in the novel. Quetzalcoatl is clearly associated with the Lunas because of his affiliations with farming, priests, and knowledge. The Lunas prize these qualities above all others and hope that Antonio will become a man of learning and a farmer priest. Tezcatlipoca is less clearly related to the Marez family, but the god's association with wind, the earth, and turmoil does link him to the wild vaqueros of Gabriel's family with their penchant for wandering all over the world. In addition, Tezcatlipoca's competition with Quetzalcoatl over the ownership of the world is comparative to the rift that develops between the Lunas and Marez over who will "rule" Antonio's future. By the end of the book, however, the conflict between the two families is largely overcome; Gabriel Marez admits that the time of the vaqueros is ending and that Antonio should choose his own path by taking the best qualities of both backgrounds. In the same way, the decision for Tezcatlipoca and Quetzalcoatl to rule over the world in a partnership seems to demonstrate an acceptance of a shared responsibility and a return to balance.

Anaya's decision to incorporate Aztec myths to such an extent in his novel demonstrates the significant role that these myths still play in Mexican culture. Throughout the novel, Antonio struggles to reconcile all of the clashing beliefs that he encounters, and one of the most difficult rifts is between the American culture he experiences at school and the Mexican culture that he experiences at home. By infusing his novel with this Aztec cultural history, Anaya gives his readers more insight into Chicano culture and adds more depth and history to the characters and conflicts that he describes in his writing.

                                    Aztec Mythology in Bless Me, Ultima

Author of ClassicNote and Sources

Caitlin Vincent, author of ClassicNote. Completed on April 20, 2008, copyright held by GradeSaver.

Updated and revised Soman Chainani June 27, 2008. Copyright held by GradeSaver.

Margarite Fernadez Olmos. Rudolfo A. Anaya: A Critical Companion. Westport: Greenwood Press, 1999.

Abelardo Baeza. Man of Aztlan: A Biography of Rudolfo Anaya. Waco: Eakin Press, 2001.

Edwin Adams Davis. Of the Night Wind's Telling: Legends from the Valley of Mexico. Norman: University of Oklahoma Press, 1976.

Miguel Leon-Portilla. Aztec Thought and Culture: A Study of the Ancient Nahuatl Mind. Norman: University of Oklahoma Press, 1990.

Dianne Klein, "Coming of Age in Novels by Rudolfo Anaya and Sandra Cisneros," in The English Journal, Vol. 81, No. 5. (Sept. 1992), pp. 21-26.

Enrique R. Lamadrid, "Myth as the Cognitive Process of Popular Culture in Rudolfo Anaya's Bless Me, Ultima: The Dialect of Knowledge," in Hispania, Vol. 68, No. 3. (Sept. 1985), pp. 496-501.

Theresa M. Kanoza, "The Golden Carp and Moby Dick: Rudolfo Anaya's Multi-Culturalism," in MELUS, Vol. 24, No. 2. (Summer 1999), pp. 159-171.

Thomas Vallegos, "Ritual Process and the Family in the Chicano Novel," in MELUS, Vol. 10, No. 4. (Winter 1983), pp. 5-16.

Paul Beekman Taylor, "The Chicano Translation of Troy: Epic Topoi in the Novels of Rudolfo A. Anaya," in MELUS, Vol. 19, No. 3. (Autumn 1994), pp. 19-35.

Manuel Villar Raso and Maria Herrera-Sobek, "A Spanish Novelist's Perspective on Chicano/a Literature," in the Journal of Modern Literature, Vol. 25, No. 1. (Fall 2001), pp. 17-34.

Quiz 1

1. How old is Antonio when the novel begins?
- A. ten
- B. six
- C. eight
- D. seven

2. Who first takes Antonio to see the golden carp?
- A. Ultima
- B. Narciso
- C. Florence
- D. Cico

3. What is a vaquero?
- A. A drunk
- B. A cowboy
- C. A bird
- D. A prostitute

4. Which character drowns after a swimming accident?
- A. Samuel
- B. Antonio
- C. Florence
- D. Cico

5. Who is the fastest runner in town?
- A. Samuel
- B. The Vitamin Kid
- C. Antonio
- D. Horse

6. Who kills Narciso?
- A. Ultima
- B. Lupito
- C. Gabriel
- D. Tenorio

7. Where are Antonio's brothers at the beginning of the novel?
   A. Studying at the University
   B. Working in California
   C. Farming with the Lunas
   D. Fighting in World War II

8. What language does Antonio speak at home?
   A. Navajo
   B. English
   C. Spanish
   D. French

9. Which character does not believe in God?
   A. Samuel
   B. Antonio
   C. Florence
   D. Maria

10. What does Antonio's mother want him to be when he grows up?
   A. A healer
   B. A priest
   C. A vaquero
   D. A school teacher

11. Where does Gabriel want to live?
   A. Mexico
   B. California
   C. Spain
   D. Albuquerque

12. What kind of animal is Ultima's familiar?
   A. A horse
   B. A hawk
   C. An owl
   D. A golden carp

13. **Who is Antonio's first grade teacher?**
    A. Ultima
    B. Miss Violet
    C. Rosie
    D. Miss Maestas

14. **Where does Antonio sleep?**
    A. In the attic
    B. In the stable
    C. In the closet
    D. In the spare bedroom

15. **What is a llano?**
    A. A type of mountain
    B. A type of medicine used by Ultima
    C. a New Mexican legend
    D. A large, grassy plain

16. **Who delivered Antonio when he was born?**
    A. Ultima
    B. Deborah
    C. Maria
    D. Rosie

17. **What does Ultima teach Antonio on their walks together?**
    A. The names of plants and herbs
    B. Witchcraft
    C. Catholic doctrine
    D. How to speak English

18. **Who kills Lupito?**
    A. The mob
    B. Ultima
    C. Gabriel
    D. The sheriff

19. **Who kills the sheriff?**
    A. Lupito
    B. Gabriel
    C. Narciso
    D. Tenorio

20. **What is Narciso known as?**
    A. A drunk
    B. A healer
    C. A singer
    D. A cowboy

21. **What does the yerba del manso NOT cure?**
    A. Colic in babies
    B. Burns
    C. Sores
    D. Broken bones

22. **Who takes Antonio to pick apples with the Lunas?**
    A. Ultima
    B. Gabriel
    C. Uncle Lucas
    D. Uncle Pedro

23. **What does Ultima say Antonio will be when he grows up?**
    A. A farmer
    B. A priest
    C. A vaquero
    D. A man of learning

24. **Where do Andrew, León, and Eugene meet before coming home after the war?**
    A. San Francisco
    B. London
    C. San Diego
    D. Mexico City

25. **Why did Lupito kill the sheriff?**
    A. He wanted to marry the sheriff's daughter
    B. He was suffering from war sickness
    C. He owed the sheriff money
    D. He was drunk

Quiz 1 Answer Key

1. **(B)** six
2. **(D)** Cico
3. **(B)** A cowboy
4. **(C)** Florence
5. **(B)** The Vitamin Kid
6. **(D)** Tenorio
7. **(D)** Fighting in World War II
8. **(C)** Spanish
9. **(C)** Florence
10. **(B)** A priest
11. **(B)** California
12. **(C)** An owl
13. **(D)** Miss Maestas
14. **(A)** In the attic
15. **(D)** A large, grassy plain
16. **(A)** Ultima
17. **(A)** The names of plants and herbs
18. **(A)** The mob
19. **(A)** Lupito
20. **(A)** A drunk
21. **(D)** Broken bones
22. **(D)** Uncle Pedro
23. **(D)** A man of learning
24. **(C)** San Diego
25. **(B)** He was suffering from war sickness

Quiz 2

1. Who first tells Antonio the story of the Golden Carp?
A. Samuel
B. Ultima
C. Cico
D. Horse

2. Who bewitches Uncle Lucas?
A. Ultima
B. Gabriel
C. Tenorio
D. The three Trementina sisters

3. What is a bruja?
A. A witch
B. A healer
C. A singer
D. A prostitute

4. Who was Ultima's teacher?
A. Father Byrnes
B. The flying man
C. The Golden Carp
D. Tenorio

5. Who tends a beautiful garden beyond the river?
A. Ultima
B. Gabriel
C. Narciso
D. Cico

6. What is the enemy of the Golden Carp?
A. Ultima
B. The black bass
C. Narciso
D. Tenorio

7. **What does Márez mean?**
    A. Sea
    B. Air
    C. Blood
    D. Horse

8. **Which language does Antonio's sisters prefer to speak?**
    A. Navajo
    B. Italian
    C. English
    D. Spanish

9. **What is Antonio forbidden to touch in Ultima's room?**
    A. The owl
    B. The books
    C. The herbs and medicines
    D. The three clay dolls on her shelf

10. **What does Ultima give Antonio to protect him?**
    A. Her owl
    B. Her magic herbs
    C. Her three dolls
    D. Her scapular

11. **Why does Antonio's mother tolerate Narciso?**
    A. Because he used to work with her father
    B. Because he took Antonio fishing
    C. Because he helped her when her twins were born
    D. Because he is lonely

12. **Who claims to have proof that Ultima is a witch?**
    A. Lupito
    B. Narciso
    C. Antonio
    D. Tenorio

13. **What is the test for witchcraft?**
     A. Mark a doorway with a cross made from holy needles and make the accused walk through it
     B. Throw holy water on the accused
     C. Send the accused to give confession at church
     D. Mark a doorway with holy water and make the accused walk through it

14. **How does Tenorio lose an eye?**
     A. Ultima's owl attacks him
     B. Ultima attacks him
     C. Narciso attacks him
     D. Antonio attacks him

15. **What is the coffin of the Trementina witch made out of?**
     A. Pine branches
     B. Cottonwood branches
     C. Oak branches
     D. Fir branches

16. **Who invites Antonio to work on the farm with the Lunas during the summer?**
     A. Uncle Juan
     B. Prudencio
     C. Uncle Mateo
     D. Uncle Lucas

17. **Who is Antonio's third grade teacher?**
     A. Andrew
     B. Deborah
     C. Miss Violet
     D. Miss Maestas

18. **Who wets his pants during the Christmas play?**
     A. Samuel
     B. Antonio
     C. Abel
     D. Horse

19. **Who plays the Virgin Mary in the Christmas play?**
    A. Florence
    B. Cico
    C. Horse
    D. Lloyd

20. **Who does Antonio find at Rosie's when he follows Narciso?**
    A. Andrew
    B. Gabriel
    C. Tenorio
    D. Uncle Lucas

21. **What does Antonio pray for Lupito while he is dying?**
    A. A prayer of petition
    B. An Act of Charity
    C. An Act of Love
    D. An Act of Contrition

22. **What happens to Antonio after Narciso is killed?**
    A. He is arrested
    B. He is sent to California
    C. He gets pneumonia
    D. He tries to run away

23. **Where is Narciso killed by Tenorio?**
    A. In Rosie's
    B. Under the juniper tree
    C. On the llano
    D. Outside the church

24. **Why did Narciso turn to drink?**
    A. He lost his job
    B. His parents died in the diptheria epidemic
    C. His friends died in World War II
    D. His wife died in the diptheria epidemic

25. **What happened to the car that Eugene and León bought?**
    A. They drove it into the river
    B. They burned it to keep warm in the blizzard
    C. They left it at home
    D. They wrecked it in an accident with another car

Quiz 2 Answer Key

1. **(A)** Samuel
2. **(D)** The three Trementina sisters
3. **(A)** A witch
4. **(B)** The flying man
5. **(C)** Narciso
6. **(B)** The black bass
7. **(A)** Sea
8. **(C)** English
9. **(D)** The three clay dolls on her shelf
10. **(D)** Her scapular
11. **(C)** Because he helped her when her twins were born
12. **(D)** Tenorio
13. **(A)** Mark a doorway with a cross made from holy needles and make the accused walk through it
14. **(A)** Ultima's owl attacks him
15. **(B)** Cottonwood branches
16. **(A)** Uncle Juan
17. **(C)** Miss Violet
18. **(C)** Abel
19. **(C)** Horse
20. **(A)** Andrew
21. **(D)** An Act of Contrition
22. **(C)** He gets pneumonia
23. **(B)** Under the juniper tree
24. **(D)** His wife died in the diptheria epidemic
25. **(B)** They burned it to keep warm in the blizzard

Quiz 3

1. **Where did Eugene and León go after they left home?**
   A. San Francisco
   B. San Diego
   C. Las Vegas
   D. Albuquerque

2. **Who do Eugene and León take with them with they leave again?**
   A. Andrew
   B. Deborah
   C. Gabriel
   D. Antonio

3. **Who kills Ultima's owl?**
   A. Gabriel
   B. Antonio
   C. Tenorio
   D. Cico

4. **Where do Florence's sisters work?**
   A. At Allen's Market
   B. At Rosie's
   C. At the church
   D. At the school

5. **What did Antonio have to do to pass his catechism test?**
   A. Recite the Our Father
   B. Explain what happens to people who die with a mortal sin on their soul
   C. Explain the miracle of the Virgin Mary
   D. Recite the Apostle's Creed

6. **Who refuses to confess his sins to Antonio?**
   A. Florence
   B. Abel
   C. Bones
   D. Horse

7. **How do Antonio's friends punish him for being a "bad priest"?**
    A. The Indian torture
    B. They give him a bloody nose
    C. They refuse to speak to him
    D. They throw his jacket in the ditch

8. **How does Tenorio kill Ultima?**
    A. He kills her owl
    B. He suffocates her
    C. He stabs her
    D. He shoots her

9. **What does Antonio hear from God after his first communion?**
    A. Nothing
    B. "I am the one true God"
    C. "Everything happens for a reason"
    D. "Know thyself"

10. **What falls from the sky onto Téllez's house?**
    A. Stones
    B. Locusts
    C. Hail
    D. Frogs

11. **Who is the narrator of the book?**
    A. Ultima
    B. Gabriel
    C. Antonio as a child
    D. Antonio as an adult

12. **Where is the book set?**
    A. Guadalupe, New Mexico
    B. Santa Fe, New Mexico
    C. Pastura, New Mexico
    D. San Diego, California

13. **Which event in Antonio's life spurs his questions about sin and punishment?**
   - A. Ultima's death
   - B. Lupito's death
   - C. Narciso's death
   - D. Tenorio's death

14. **Why does Antonio want to show Florence the Golden Carp?**
   - A. So that he will take his sisters away from Rosie's brothel
   - B. So that he will prefer Antonio to his other friends
   - C. So that he has something to believe in
   - D. So that he will go fishing with him

15. **What does Ultima charge Téllez for removing the curse on his house?**
   - A. Incense
   - B. Several pieces of gold
   - C. Several pieces of silver
   - D. A lamb

16. **In Antonio's dream, what does he use to bait his fishing hooks?**
   - A. The Golden Carp
   - B. Ultima's owl
   - C. Worms
   - D. The livers of his brothers

17. **In Antonio's final dream, what do the priests pour on the altar?**
   - A. Water from the river
   - B. Pigeon's blood
   - C. Goat's milk
   - D. Wine

18. **What rules almost every part of the life of a Luna?**
   - A. The sun
   - B. The moon
   - C. God
   - D. The harvest

19. **What does Antonio eventually come to recognize the owl to be?**
    A. Ultima's magic power
    B. Tenorio's magic power
    C. The protective spirit of God
    D. The protective spirit of Ultima

20. **What is the owl NOT the spirit of?**
    A. Ultima
    B. The Golden Carp
    C. The night and the moon
    D. The llano

21. **Who kills Tenorio?**
    A. Ultima
    B. Antonio
    C. Uncle Lucas
    D. Uncle Pedro

22. **Where does Antonio bury the owl?**
    A. Under a forked juniper tree
    B. In the church cemetery
    C. Next to the river
    D. On the llano

23. **Which of Antonio's friends is a Protestant?**
    A. Samuel
    B. Red
    C. Bones
    D. Horse

24. **According to Antonio's parents, why are his brothers restless?**
    A. Because of the war sickness
    B. Because they were meant to be Lunas
    C. Because they are poor
    D. Because of their MÃ¡rez blood

25. **Where does Andrew work in town?**
   A. On the highway
   B. At Allen's Market
   C. At Rosie's
   D. At the bar

Quiz 3 Answer Key

1. **(C)** Las Vegas
2. **(A)** Andrew
3. **(C)** Tenorio
4. **(B)** At Rosie's
5. **(D)** Recite the Apostle's Creed
6. **(A)** Florence
7. **(A)** The Indian torture
8. **(A)** He kills her owl
9. **(A)** Nothing
10. **(A)** Stones
11. **(D)** Antonio as an adult
12. **(A)** Guadalupe, New Mexico
13. **(B)** Lupito's death
14. **(C)** So that he has something to believe in
15. **(D)** A lamb
16. **(D)** The livers of his brothers
17. **(B)** Pigeon's blood
18. **(B)** The moon
19. **(D)** The protective spirit of Ultima
20. **(B)** The Golden Carp
21. **(D)** Uncle Pedro
22. **(A)** Under a forked juniper tree
23. **(B)** Red
24. **(D)** Because of their Márez blood
25. **(B)** At Allen's Market

Quiz 4

1. **How do Antonio's brothers spend their service money when they return?**
    A. They gamble at the Eight Ball Pool Hall
    B. They open a restaurant
    C. They buy expensive cars and clothing
    D. They buy land on the llano

2. **Who is the "leader" of Antonio's three brothers?**
    A. Eugene
    B. Andrew
    C. Gabriel
    D. LeÃ³n

3. **What does the Vitamin Kid call Antonio when he races past him?**
    A. The loser
    B. The giant killer
    C. The farmer
    D. The priest

4. **Why is it bad luck to fish for the brown carp in the river?**
    A. Because they are poisonous
    B. Because they were once the people of the land
    C. Because they are owned by a wealthy man who lives upstream
    D. Because they are magical

5. **According to Samuel, what is the Golden Carp?**
    A. An angel who protects the people in the community
    B. A monster
    C. A god who loved the people of the land so much that he turned into a
carp to protect them
    D. A demon

6. **What does Uncle Lucas cough up after Ultima's treatment?**
    A. A juniper branch
    B. A frog
    C. A ball of hair
    D. A snake

7. **What is Ultima's alternate name to the Márez family?**
   A. La Bruja
   B. La Grande
   C. Esperanza
   D. Madre

8. **What is a curandera?**
   A. A witch
   B. An ancient priestess
   C. A cowboy
   D. A woman who practices folk medicine

9. **How much does Ultima charge Prudencio Luna to cure his son?**
   A. Forty dollars
   B. A bushel of vegetables
   C. Fifty pieces of silver
   D. A lamb

10. **What animals represent the Trementina sisters?**
    A. Wolves
    B. Dragons
    C. Coyotes
    D. Frogs

11. **What does Ultima do with the living ball of hair that Uncle Lucas vomits up?**
    A. She puts it on her shelf at home
    B. She leaves it at the house of the Trementina sisters
    C. She stabs it and buries it
    D. She burns it

12. **What does Antonio find on the ground after the mob tests Ultima for witchcraft?**
    A. An owl feather
    B. The three dolls
    C. Ultima's scapular
    D. The cross made from holy needles

13. **What is the first line of the novel?**
    A. "Let me begin at the beginning"
    B. "Ultima came to stay with us the summer I was almost seven"
    C. "Time stood still, and it shared with me all that had been, and all that was to come..."
    D. "The sun was white in the bright blue sky"

14. **What kind of novel is Bless Me, Ultima?**
    A. An allegorical novel
    B. A utopian novel
    C. A bildungsroman
    D. A pastoral novel

15. **How Antonio help Ultima to cure Uncle Lucas?**
    A. He does the chores around the house
    B. He keeps Ultima company
    C. He nurses his uncle back to health
    D. He serves as a medium

16. **How does Ultima resolve the conflict between the two families when Antonio is born?**
    A. She declares that he will become a vaquero
    B. She declares that she alone will know his destiny
    C. She declares that he will become a priest
    D. She declares that he will abandon both families

17. **How does Antonio reconcile the seeming conflict between innocence and sex?**
    A. He decides to become a priest as soon as possible
    B. He discovers that his ancestor, the Luna priest, was not celibate and that innocence and sex are not mutually exclusive
    C. He denounces his brothers for their constant lust
    D. He decides that he could never be a priest

18. **What does the term "chicano" mean?**
    A. Magical
    B. Mexican American
    C. A type of horse that roams on the llano
    D. A type of song sung in New Mexico

19. **Which characters personify the struggle between good and evil in the novel?**
    A. Narcisco and Tenorio
    B. Ultima and Narciso
    C. Ultima and Tenorio
    D. Antonio and Tenorio

20. **In Antonio's first dream, what do the Luna rub on Antonio's forehead as a baby?**
    A. Baptismal oil
    B. Water from the river valley
    C. Corn from the river valley
    D. Soil from the river valley

21. **How do the Márez want to dispose of Antonio's umbilical cord?**
    A. They want to release it in the river
    B. They want to feed it to their horses
    C. They want to bury it in the fields
    D. They want to burn it and scatter the ashes on the llano

22. **What epiphany does Ultima reveal to Antonio in a dream?**
    A. There is no God
    B. The two waters are one
    C. The Golden Carp is going to bring about the apocalyse
    D. God punishes both the wicked and the good

23. **Why is Narciso's murderer unpunished?**
    A. The town never found Narciso's body
    B. The coroner decided that Narciso's death was accidental
    C. The townspeople were happy Narciso was dead
    D. Narciso's family decided not to press charges

24. **How does Antonio's father feel about living in Guadalupe?**
    A. He doesn't care where they live
    B. He loves the town
    C. He wants to run for Mayor
    D. He hates it and misses the llano

25. **After witnessing Lupito's death, how does Antonio feel when he hears
    the owl?**
    A. He is comforted
    B. He is irritated
    C. He becomes even more frightened
    D. He reminds himself that he needs to go hunting

Quiz 4 Answer Key

1. **(A)** They gamble at the Eight Ball Pool Hall
2. **(A)** Eugene
3. **(B)** The giant killer
4. **(B)** Because they were once the people of the land
5. **(C)** A god who loved the people of the land so much that he turned into a carp to protect them
6. **(C)** A ball of hair
7. **(B)** La Grande
8. **(D)** A woman who practices folk medicine
9. **(A)** Forty dollars
10. **(C)** Coyotes
11. **(D)** She burns it
12. **(D)** The cross made from holy needles
13. **(B)** "Ultima came to stay with us the summer I was almost seven"
14. **(C)** A bildungsroman
15. **(D)** He serves as a medium
16. **(B)** She declares that she alone will know his destiny
17. **(B)** He discovers that his ancestor, the Luna priest, was not celibate and that innocence and sex are not mutually exclusive
18. **(B)** Mexican American
19. **(C)** Ultima and Tenorio
20. **(D)** Soil from the river valley
21. **(D)** They want to burn it and scatter the ashes on the llano
22. **(B)** The two waters are one
23. **(B)** The coroner decided that Narciso's death was accidental
24. **(D)** He hates it and misses the llano
25. **(A)** He is comforted

1734413

Made in the USA